"This book demystifies social media, explains useful measuring tools and suggests different ways to make data-driven decisions on social media investments. For companies considering social media or new to it, it provides a clearly written, easy to follow, practical introduction. For companies with an established social media presence, like Electrolux, it provides simple, matter-of-fact ways to explain social media impact to others within the organization."
MayKay Kopf, Chief Marketing Officer, Electrolux

"Social media has gone from curiosity to critical business communications tool. However many companies still aren't applying meaningful measures to their social media strategies. Holloman's latest book offers practical social media ROI advice and is packed with real-world examples that will benefit companies of all sizes."
Jeremy Woolf, Global Digital and Social Media Lead for Text100 Global Communications

"Business has gone social media crazy, but measuring ROI is still something of a Holy Grail – how do you do it, how do you prove the value of your activity on the bottom-line and how do you use the feedback to convince the social media detractors in your organization? Christer's book lifts the lid on this 'dark art', explains why it matters and offers real hands-on guidance to implementing meaningful ways for measuring ROI."
Paul Beadle, Head of Social Media, Nationwide Building Society

"This is a solid introduction to measuring the impact of social media; an essential element for anybody seeking to unlock the potential of social business or to affect a full digital transformation of their organization. Another excellent book from Christer Holloman with insightful and practical guidance."
Blake Cahill, Global Head of Digital & Social Marketing for Royal Philips

"The external question that anyone who has a professional association with social media gets asked is, 'what return can I expect from getting involved?'. While answers given tend to range from the sublime to the ridiculous, this book gives a sound basis for making a business case for

investing in social media related programs. As ever with Christer's books, he has painstakingly taken the time to source case studies from organizations that are leading the way. If you're looking to take a more business-like approach to your social media efforts, this book is certainly for you."
Eb Adeyeri, Digital Communications Consultant, Strategy Director, We Are Social

"This book goes far beyond measuring 'likes' and 'followers'. It gives straightforward advice on how to ensure social media influences the very bottom line of your business, and as this is the conversation that CEO/ stakeholders are expecting, this is the book for you. With the clarity in explanation it provides guidelines, tools and case-studies, to take the guesswork out of understanding the impact of social collaboration and provides the 'north star' to measure and reflects its ROI."
Prithvi Shergill, Chief Human Resources Officer, HCL

"As Social Media marketing moves out of its more youthful stages and squarely into adolescence, once experimental forays in brand engagement now require concrete approaches in determining the value of those efforts. Christer, as usual, brings the latest thinking from a variety of experts in the field. It's a remarkable and much needed contribution to the marketing discipline as a whole."
Alex Yenni, Strategy Director, Blast Radius

"If you began a social media program because you were worried you'd be late to the conversation, *The Social Media MBA Guide to ROI* is an important tool to convert those new found cyber fans into a real life, bottom line, impact. A must for any company strategy."
Jim Ibister, General Manager, RiverCentre, VP Facility Administration, Minnesota Wild

"In the constantly evolving space that is social media, Christer offers a laser-like focus on key case studies and best practices from around the globe that will help business leaders connect with their audience and achieve maximum results from their programs and efforts."
Jenni Butler, Product Line Manager-Mixers, Hobart Corporation

THE SOCIAL MEDIA
MBA GUIDE TO ROI

tHE SOCIAL mEDIA MBA Guide to ROI

How to measure and improve your return on investment

Christer Holloman

WILEY

First published in 2014

© 2014 Christer Holloman

Registered office

John Wiley and Sons Ltd, The Atrium, Southern Gate, Chichester, West Sussex, PO19 8SQ, United Kingdom

For details of our global editorial offices, for customer services and for information about how to apply for permission to reuse the copyright material in this book please see our website at www.wiley.com.

Wiley publishes in a variety of print and electronic formats and by print-on-demand. Some material included with standard print versions of this book may not be included in e-books or in print-on-demand. If this book refers to media such as a CD or DVD that is not included in the version you purchased, you may download this material at http://booksupport.wiley.com. For more information about Wiley products, visit www.wiley.com.

Designations used by companies to distinguish their products are often claimed as trademarks. All brand names and product names used in this book and on its cover are trade names, service marks, trademark or registered trademarks of their respective owners. The publisher and the book are not associated with any product or vendor mentioned in this book. None of the companies referenced within the book have endorsed the book.

Limit of Liability/Disclaimer of Warranty: While the publisher and author have used their best efforts in preparing this book, they make no representations or warranties with the respect to the accuracy or completeness of the contents of this book and specifically disclaim any implied warranties of merchantability or fitness for a particular purpose. It is sold on the understanding that the publisher is not engaged in rendering professional services and neither the publisher nor the author shall be liable for damages arising herefrom. If professional advice or other expert assistance is required, the services of a competent professional should be sought.

A catalogue record for this book is available from the Library of Congress

A catalogue record for this book is available from the British Library.

ISBN 978-1-118-84439-7 (hardback)   ISBN 978-1-118-89829-1 (ebk)
ISBN 978-1-118-84441-0 (ebk)

Cover design: Rawshock Design

Set in 11.5/15.5pt FF Scala by Toppan Best-set Premedia Limited, Hong Kong
Printed in Great Britain by TJ International Ltd, Padstow, Cornwall, UK

CONTENTS

ACKNOWLEDGEMENTS

I dedicate this book to (in alphabetical order):

Aaro Murpy, Adam Regan, Anders Hallsten, Andreas Mentzer, Besfort Williams, Christoffer Harlos, Dan Jexin, Hugh Currie, James Baker, John Philip, Jonathan Touvinen, Kaj Alftan, Lary Rutzenholtsz, Ludvig Freij, Quim Cosp, Robert Downer, Robert Malton and Stefan Kuris.

You have made quite an impression on me, I feel privileged to have made your acquaintance.

Thanks for all the many happy memories so far, and all those still to come!

PREFACE

Anyone can make things complicated; it takes real talent to make something look simple.

With the publication of this book, the total number of "students" to have "enrolled" in *The Social Media MBA* "course" is on track to surpass 10,000 individuals by the end of this year; that's not even including the thousands of business professionals I've met in person while travelling around giving talks on this topic during the last few years.

Do not miss out on the opportunity to connect and network with fellow alumni by joining the "The Social Media MBA Alumni" group on LinkedIn, just google it. It's a great and safe place to eavesdrop on interesting conversations, ask questions, exchange ideas or perhaps look around for new job openings or recruit a member to your team. Sign up now before you forget! Use it as a support resource as you continue reading this book and start applying it in practice.

The original *The Social Media MBA* was published a little over two years ago. An Amazon bestseller that at its peak was one of the 500 most bought books of all the 6.2 million books on sale in the UK, and it was in the Top 5 within its category for six consecutive months. Now available in different languages, it has remained steady in the Top 10 in several markets; an extraordinary achievement considering the speed of change in this field and the sheer number of new books and articles published on this topic every month. For me it is a testament to the strategic decision to intentionally position this book series as one for those that already "get" social media but want to elevate their application to the next level. I let other writers deal with the entry-level stuff. The fact that two years on, people are still learning new things by reading the first book, tells me I have been successful in capturing leading thinking that is standing the test of time and helping practitioners like you to look smart and impress your peers.

When I'm invited to talk about social media, 9 times out of 10, people most frequently request that I share best practise case studies to inspire the development and delivery of their own social media strategy. Reading the reviews of the first book, it also becomes clear that one of its most appreciated aspects is the handful of case studies I featured in it. I decided to address the unwavering demand head on.

Last year a unique collection of 25 case studies showcasing the best business use of social media was published in *The Social Media MBA in Practice* and it was extremely well received. One of the chief reasons being that it really pushed the boundaries of what previously and traditionally had been defined as classic social media territory. I started the book by saying that if social is owned by marketing, marketing isn't being very social. This has been one of my key messages on the speaking circuit ever since. Making each department adopt a social media mindset is the new frontier for social media, not how to come up with a new viral video or count the number of "likes". The cases I selected and developed bring to life the idea that social is not just a tool for marketing and PR, but indeed for the entire organization. We read about cases as wide ranging as how the Israeli Foreign Office use social tools in a hostile political environment, to how the global consultancy firm PwC use internal crowdsourcing to identify new solutions to sell to clients. If the sheer breadth of those 25 case studies wasn't a clear enough message that the face of social media is changing, you get another indication that something is happening when you consider the job titles of the people that I interviewed for the book. Two years ago the people I talked to about social media had titles like "Marketing Manager" or "Community Manager". Today I'm talking social media just as much with people with titles like "Director of Product Development", "Head of Customer Service", "VP of Facility Management", "HR Director", "Quality Control Manager", etc. This is the new battleground for social media – getting social outside marketing.

I appreciate that the majority of my readers and audiences at live events, and statistically this includes you, are most likely marketing professionals, so fear not, I will have your perspective in mind throughout this entire book. Being aware of the fact that social media is being picked up and applied by departments across your organization is something you can use to your advantage. Take the high road, set up a Centre of Excellence (How? Read the Honda Europe case in *The Social Media MBA in Practice*) with heads from all departments which has or could have a social media dimension, propose yourself as the chairperson and lead from the front. By being the one that is a step ahead, the organization will naturally gravitate to you for advice and best practice. The fact that you have chosen to read this book shows that you're already on your way to solidifying that status or paving the way for it. As we will soon discover, nothing gives you more kudos further up the food chain than pushing for ROI analysis and showing your colleagues how to do it.

The book you're currently reading is independent from the first two, but if you haven't had a chance to read them yet, I would strongly urge you to consider doing it for your own benefit. It will you give you the holistic backdrop for this book, complete your collection of matching "course" books and ensure that you remain a well-rounded and well-researched social media advocate.

Christer Holloman
London, May 2014
@holloman

PS. Are you a member yet?

Don't forget the alumni network of fellow readers, people around the world that work professionally with social media. Join by searching for "The Social Media MBA Alumni" on LinkedIn. It's free of course.

HALL OF FAME

Keep an eye on what's next from the social media practitioners featured in this book:

Christer Holloman @holloman
The Social Media MBA @sm_mba

Ami Nathan @aminathan
New Business Manager at BRAVEday

Omar Johnson @beatsbydre
EVP Marketing at Beats Beats by Dr. Dre

Dee Whimp @bravedeew
Existing Business Manager at BRAVEday

Michael Gillane @bulmerscider
Brand Director at Heineken UK

Jeanette Gibson @jeanetteg
Senior Director, Social & Digital Marketing
at Cisco

Kristian Lorenzon @krislorenzon
Head of Social at O_2

Mark Rentschler   @makinomachine
Marketing Manager at Makino

Megan Peterson   @sabrehosp
Social Media Manager at Sabre

Vincent Boon   @vincentboon
Chief of Community at giffgaff

Introduction

This book is for those who want to start measuring the tangible and intangible returns on investment (ROI) on their social media activities and are looking for some straightforward advice on how to get on with it; from making the business case for social to defining suitable goals and more.

We will talk about how to set up free tools such as Google Analytics and premium tools like Radian6 to help you track ROI. We will also discuss how to make the most of the built-in ROI features on some of the most popular channels such as Facebook and YouTube.

As you will learn, social media is not just about making money but just as much about having an opportunity to save money, a less discussed aspect of ROI that we will investigate further. We will also look at how you can improve your ROI figures to help you impress your leadership team even more.

Irrespective of what industry or department you are working in, now that social media has become mainstream, your leaders will increasingly expect you to know how to measure the return on it, just as they expect you to measure the return on any other business activity you engage in. This becomes even more critical if you plan to ask for additional resources towards social, time and money, in the future.

What makes this book different?

This book aims not only to inform the marketing department on how to measure ROI, but indeed every department. We don't limit ourselves to thinking about social as "campaigns" but also as ongoing business processes. The platforms will change and methodologies become more refined, so this book won't be future proof, but at least it will steer your mind in the correct direction, one in which measuring social becomes second nature and no more strange then measuring any other company activity.

I appreciate that you have a choice of literature on this topic and of course I'm happy you picked this book, but let me tell you why I think you did the right thing. As I alluded to in the Preface, my goal is to make ROI as simple as it can possibly be. In my previous role as Head of Digital Product Development at *The Times* and *The Sunday Times*, I know first-hand that however cool a certain technical concept might be, if it's not intuitive, no one will use it and everyone will have wasted their time. I will debunk the myth that social media measuring is not possible or a "black art", I'll make it easy to understand and use.

We will not only read about the most popular models backed up by hands-on examples, but present case studies and interviews with social media leaders at some of the world's most social media savvy B2C and B2B brands, who share their first experiences. I want us to stop obsessing about "likes" and "followers" and instead talk about bottom-line value to your business.

Some authors intentionally keep things fluffy or leave key details out, either because they don't know the subject matter well enough, or because they want you to sign up to their workshops or online videos to really understand it. This book will allow you to autonomously develop a methodology to calculate the ROI of your social media efforts, whatever budgets you are working with. I firmly believe that the suggestions outlined here will help you take some of the guesswork out of your own equations and inspire you to go further.

A recent report by the US research organization Altimeter Group found that 70 per cent of businesses believed social media could meet business objectives, but only 43 per cent had a formalized strategy for how social media would meet their specific business goals. As companies invest more money in social media activities you will be put under more pressure to measure the return. To justify additional investments, more solid metrics will be required.

Ultimately, I want to inspire you to learn something new and make you so confident that you in turn, are able to teach this to others in your team and throughout your organization.

Don't forget the alumni network of fellow readers, people around the world that work professionally with social media. Join by searching for "The Social Media MBA Alumni" on LinkedIn. It's free of course.

With all that said, I think we are now set to commence class, so sharpen your pencils!

1   Strategy

Learning Objective

In this chapter I will equip you with the arguments to allow you to have a discussion with senior leaders about why and how social media and measuring it, is a requirement and not an optional extra.

This is a chapter for those of you that have to work with non-believers. If you can't convince someone that your organization should be engaging with social media there is no point in starting the conversation about ROI. If your organization is all over social media you can skip ahead to the next chapter.

Is social media for us?

You can't secure buy-in before you know the timing is right. Before you embark on your social media journey, you must start by taking a good look in the mirror and asking yourself if social media really is one for your company?

There are authors of books such as this that argue that social media is a must for every business. "If you're not on the bandwagon now, you're too late for the party!" I agree that social media is a must for every business, but only when the time is right for that particular business. The recruitment industry was early on the ball using social media for business gains, a few years later the property industry caught on but the automotive industry is still notoriously behind.

As a mentor at the tech start-up accelerator Oxygen, based at Google Campus in London, I had the privilege of getting to know the founders of a company called Carhoots.com. Today they have more followers on Pinterest then any car brand in the world, any car magazine, car show, car retailer, etc. How could a whole industry be leapfrogged by two guys working from a living room?

Which industry are you in and where on this scale is that? You will be facing different challenges depending on how mature social has become in your sector. As an early adopter, you can get away with replicating what others have done in other verticals already, as a late bloomer you have to be much more creative to make an impact.

In the same way that having a child won't save a failing marriage, embracing social media won't help a business faced with more pressing issues to address. The actual logistics of having a child is as straightforward as creating a Facebook page, but the real work begins when you have to start looking after it, this is when the problems begin. So don't do anything just for the sake of it.

Before you start spending any money on social, and therefore creating the need to monitor ROI, you should decide if this is the right time for your business. Does your business have the bandwidth to pull it off? Does it have within its DNA the willingness to try and fail and get back up again? This is very much an introspective assessment; do we know enough about social media? Why are we doing this? Is it to please a certain person? Is it scalable? Is it sustainable? Is it really what our customers want?

If the answer is "no" to any of these questions, leave it. Park social media. Go and fix other problems in your business or switch employer to one that is moving more quickly with the times.

Senior buy-in is critical for the success of your social programme, so I don't envy people who work with senior leaders that don't "get" social or who think it's something their kids do on their smartphones while watching TV. In this case, it falls upon your shoulders to educate the business on how social can improve the way you do business and instil a social mindset.

Before we progress I thought I should share with you my top tips for selling social media to your boss and any other sceptics who you might come across. First, let's examine some of the most common objections cited by businesses for staying away from social media. Then, one by one, bust the myths and surface some killer arguments that will help you win this potential battle.

Five common objections to social media by business leaders

1. Fear of the unknown

This is an objection they won't spell out, you have to read it between the lines.

My 65-year-old mother joined Facebook a few years ago and one day someone she didn't know sent her a friend request. This puzzled her, why would a stranger want to add her as a friend? She called everyone in the family asking if we knew who this person was, which we didn't. It scared her so much that she decided to permanently delete her Facebook account and would never consider another social media platform again. She will bluntly say that she fears the unknown.

Most businesspeople wouldn't be as vocal as my mother, but this is what they are basically trying to say most of the time. They don't want to lose face by admitting to not knowing something. Some even believe it will go away if they ignore it for long enough. This was certainly the case for many hotels when they realized people where reviewing them online and there wasn't anything they could do about it, or at least so they thought. Today TripAdvsior is one of the main sources of referrals for new business for many hotels and they love what social media means for them.

2. No headspace

No one wants more work, there is no free time to spend online getting more familiar with social media tools. This leads to a real lack of insight about how it actually works. Without taking the time to learn more, there will be no platform to build on. It makes sense that if you don't understand what goes in, you won't truly have a grasp of what comes out.

Keeping up with the developments in social media seems to be a full-time job in itself. The world never sleeps. The thought of keeping up with it all can be overwhelming and it's hard to know where to start. That's why you need to make it clear that you will own this space and stay on top of all the new developments for the benefit of the business. You should also have in mind a programme to disseminate information so that the business is not totally dependent on you if, one day, you decide to leave.

3. No resources

It's a fact that no company has an abundance of resource. In the last five years, many companies have reduced headcount, introduced hiring freezes or reorganized teams. When things are in a constant flux it is difficult to make a business case to set resource aside to invest in social media. This includes time and money for recruitment or retraining, implementation and sustainability. It is difficult to understand exactly what makes a good social media resource if you don't really understand the area that you expect them to excel in.

4. Nothing to say

Many aspects about social media success relate to being able to tell stories and sharing relevant content. Any self-reflecting boss would ask him- or herself if their company has enough to say. This is an objection most commonly held by B2B companies, arguing that the combination of social only being used by private consumers means that business buyers are not interested in stories. But they are and every company has stories to tell. A great example of this is Hobart and ARM featured in the first two books. Both are B2B brands that are doing exceptionally well connecting with their audiences.

5. Can't measure it

Even if you do get the resources to invest in social, how do you justify that it was a worthwhile investment? You measure it.

However, there are many that argue that you can't measure social media – and they are correct to a certain extent. As this book will point out, there is a wave of techniques that you can apply to measure this in a very precise way. By becoming familiar with them and applying them, you can prove to your boss that you can measure social just like any other form of business activity.

Instil social mindset

Having just bought this book I clearly don't have to sell the benefits of using social media to you, but you might be surprised to hear that even today, in 2014, I regularly meet businesspeople who are sceptical about using social media platforms. They most often say that social media "leaves them open and vulnerable to attacks by those who don't like something we sell or do". As if not engaging officially on social media platforms would stop that from happening anyway. (For more on this, read the case in *The Social Media MBA in Practice* about The Israeli Foreign Office).

Some sceptics are not quite as hard line as the worst offenders that write social off completely as in the example above, but they do talk about the pros and cons of social media, and I don't buy that line of reasoning either. It's like forcing yourself to list the pros and cons of having a company phone. On the one hand it's great when a customer wants to phone in an order, but on the other hand, phones cost a lot to buy and maintain. No matter how long you could make either of those lists, you wouldn't seriously consider unplugging your phones.

I worked for three years as Head of Product in Europe at one of the largest jobsites in North America called CareerBuilder.com. Owned by a large conservative newspaper conglomerate, the online side of the business which I was in, was acting like a start-up and the unofficial motto was, "act first, ask for forgiveness later"; meaning that if we saw a business opportunity, we should just go after it without waiting for approval from further up the hierarchy. This meant we could experiment with social media in a way that the mother company didn't. If you work in the latter type of slow-moving organization, then taking your own inspiration from reading this book to win them over by doing social media on the side and showing the ROI data you can extract, may not be a guarantee to make them forgive you for investing in social media efforts behind their backs. In this case, you have to take one step back and first sell social media via the official route.

Five best arguments to sell social media by business leaders

Today social has become a hygiene factor, something companies need to do in the same way they had to be in the local phone book. If you still need some killer arguments, here they are:

1. Our competitors are doing it

Just like little boys get jealous of their friends when they get a shiny new toy, businessmen in particular get just as jealous when their competitors get recognized for something they themselves are not doing, or something they have overlooked. I used to work as Head of Commercial Product development for one of the UK's largest property portals. When I joined we didn't have an iPad app, but our biggest competitor did. During my first year, the CEO finally agreed that we needed an app and at the launch he was man enough to admit that he had been too late in recognizing the opportunities apps presented. Nothing spurred him on to catch up more than seeing the competitors racing ahead.

Before you speak to your boss about getting involved in social media, spend some time creating an overview of what your three biggest competitors are doing and list things like size of fan base (even if we know that doesn't account for much, but we want to keep it simple to start with).

As a bonus to this point, it's worth noting that everyone in the office is probably doing it. If this is the case in your office, it will look the same at your prospective clients' offices too. Business is social, social is business.

2. Cheap

While there may be a recruitment or training cost, setting up social media accounts come, in the main, with no cost attached. All you need is one person and one computer, phone or tablet. How many other forms of advertising are this cost effective? Once the posts, tweets, images or videos are out in the world, they stay there. They don't become tomorrow's fish and chip paper. They are always present and they are always searchable.

This can impact on two elements of your organization's spend. Careful and well-thought-out posts can really improve organic searches and can assist your website's SEO performance. Campaigns can be run through social media and there is a real opportunity to use social media cleverly, which can lead to reducing advertising spend. Social media now becomes a little easier to sell to the board.

3. Influence opinion

Social media reaches the customer earlier in the decision-making process, making it the most valuable and true mass medium. Social media is the channel to the clients and allows you to nurture a relationship over time.

There is always something to say. When considering social media output, don't just consider what your company or organization has to say. Think about it in terms of the world. Keep an eye on the news. A pencil company can congratulate pupils on exam results day. A religious organization can consider the implications of a breakthrough at the CERN physics facility in Switzerland.

4. Become the non-corporate face of the company

Social media is a great way to connect one-on-one with your customers. Trusted social media colleagues can be relied to post as @themselves. There are many benefits to engaging with your customers in this way.

Allowing customers to forge a relationship with the people behind the company allows the customers to build a stronger connection with, and sense of belonging to, one another. Most social media interaction takes place on mobile devices. These are more likely to be owned personally, which strengthens the feeling that you are hand-in-hand with the people you are speaking to.

It allows you to develop a deeper emotional relationship with the customers and to develop an empathetic understanding of their situation. This is critical for customer loyalty and creating an enduring relationship with them.

5. Improved customer relations

Although similar to the point above, it is different in the detail. Being "live" on social media will allow you to "harness the negative" and turn it to your advantage. So many times, customers post and tweet about poor service or products and will continue to, regardless of your organization's stance on social media.

Seize the opportunity to turn a perceived failure into a success. Stephen Fry took to Twitter to complain about his Blackberry. Blackberry approached him publicly through social media and dealt with the problem out in the open. Who won that one? Everyone. Stephen got his problem sorted and Blackberry was able to swoop in like a knight on a white horse.

Word of mouth is very powerful on social media. Not only do you get to engage with your customers but it will unlock the door for you to discover their friends and contacts – social networking at its optimum.

So, in conclusion, when selling this to your leaders, don't make it sound like you're forcing it down their throats, but do make them think it was their idea. You want them to give you the mandate to get on with it!

What is ROI?

It's time to talk about the elephant in the room. Before we get into the details of measuring ROI (Return on Investment), I want to make sure we are all on the same page with regards to what we are talking about.

ROI is traditionally a financial equation to show the sales delivered from the cost of making that sale; production cost, marketing spend etc. It is a cut and dried equation that has a simple linear nature. This is unlike social media, where a "tipping point" can be much harder to identify.

When I give talks about social media I try to avoid using the words Facebook and Twitter, and over 4,000 words into this book, I've only mentioned these once or twice. For me social media is something much bigger than individual platforms, even though we are zeroing in on some platform-specific matrices in this book, ROI can be applied to any business processes that are driven by a social media mythology and not limited to a set of consumer websites. A good example of this is Electrolux who use social media tools to capture ideas for business improvement from staff. The methodologies you will learn here can be adjusted to work around your company-specific social media activity and goals.

The R and the I

In order to deliver on your ROI targets you need to be clear what success looks like, what is R for your business? For example:

- Acquire customers more cheaply?
- Reduce costs linked to your operation?
- Explore a new route to market?
- Improve the way you service your customer?

Depending on what your R is you can choose the most relevant I, for example:

- What sort of people resource do we need to put in place to support this?

- How much money are we investing?
- What's the time frame we are working towards?

Once you have established the R and the I you can concentrate on execution.

That is to say:

(Money gained from activity − cost of activity)/cost of activity = ROI

You will receive a number. If you want to understand your ROI as a percentage, multiply your ROI figure by 100.

KPIs

In addition to ROI you can also choose to use Key Performance Indicators (KPIs) to monitor specific areas of your overall social activity. Again, depending on the nature of your business and your goals, different KPIs should be used. Below are some examples suitable for different activities.

Figure 1.1: Advocacy KPIs

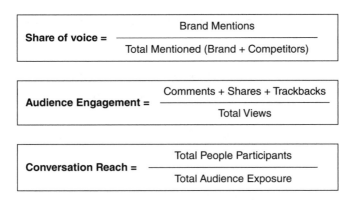

Figure 1.2: Dialog KPIs

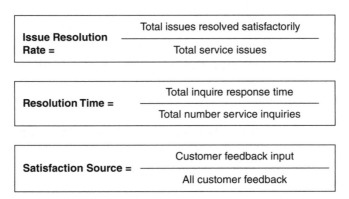

Figure 1.3: Support KPIs

Can you measure?

Even if you or your superiors or predecessors have managed to successfully sell-in the absolute necessity of doing something in the social sphere, the next step in proposing to measure social media can be controversial for various reasons. There are a lot of people who say you can't measure social media, so here are some of the arguments you might come across and should be prepared to address.

1. There are too many entry points for us to determine the key interaction

We can take an overview of what is happening on social media channels. This will provide analytics that we can make assumptions from, but the element of guesswork is too high to deem it scientific or mathematic. When was the last time you bought something on the back of reading a tweet?

We can take measurements from the key social media channels and even extend that to lesser-used and emerging channels. However, we are unable to access all sharing hotspots, and sharing is a key element to social media. Email and Instant Messaging are also key sharing formats, but they are private and impenetrable. This means we are unable to pinpoint the exact point of brand or product buy-in.

2. Social media is not a transaction, it's a relationship

Social media is not where the action happens. Social media is a space where conversations begin. It is a useful tool to take measurements of brand awareness from, but it will never deliver the bottom line number we seek.

We can measure certain elements of the customer interaction through social media.

Awareness

The key awareness metric can be ascertained by assessing if more people know about your brand than they did previously. This figure can be reached by taking brand mentions, brand proposition mentions, positive mentions and share of voice. Share of voice is the number of brand mentions divided by the total number of your industry mentions. Industry mentions is the total number of your brand mentions plus your competitors. Once you reach this number, you compare it against the previous period. This figure cannot specify if any financial transaction has taken place at this point and so cannot be considered an ROI metric.

Reach

Reach can be considered as knowing how many people can hear what your brand is saying. This figure can be generated by calculating the rise in followers or fans in a given time period. This will also require some social media analytics tools to demonstrate the geographical information of the users. These tools include Facebook Insights and LinkedIn analytics.

Traffic

Are your posts bringing people to your website? When you broadcast or publish through your social media channels, are you driving traffic to your website or are your posts missing the mark? Google Analytics will produce reports to show you where your website customers are coming from, but not necessarily why. This means that you cannot identify a sales lead that was generated as a direct result of your post.

Engagement

If you join traffic with click-through rates, you will understand what impact your output is having on your customers. You will be able to look at "likes", shares, retweets and positive buzz created by your activity. This is like laying one layer on top of another. You will see a picture, but not a complete end-to-end customer journey relating to one user.

Intelligence

What are they saying and how are your followers reacting to you? This type of information is useful and interesting, but it can act like a massive disparate focus group to capture the general mood of your audience. It would not be common practice to generate an ROI figure on the basis of market research.

To calculate ROI, you need to understand the relationship between the money that you have spent against the money you have gained as a consequence of your activity (investment).

3. What are you measuring with ROI?

When considering ROI, what will you do with the eventual figure? Is it to determine the impact of your investment for your brand or product? Or is it to understand how well your social media is performing against the other channels in your marketing strategy e.g. advertising, email, pay per click. Is it to understand how you will build your next marketing plan and how to allocate your budget?

This is not as scientific as it may seem, despite the fact that a mathematical equation is involved. Social media is a communications tool which is in a constant state of flux and growth. The social media space is rich with newcomers on an annual basis. It is also full of the almost-rans; those who have not scaled the heights of Twitter, Facebook and YouTube, but are by no means defunct. The third group concerns those who do a similar job (sharing, favourites etc.) and who have loyal followers but who will never have a tipping point of followers because they operate in a saturated marketplace.

It also does not follow that you can throw more investment at social media to see a greater return. There comes a point where too many posts or interactivity can cause customers to become overwhelmed.

4. Calculating your investment

What costs should you include when assessing your investment, which costs would you have had anyway? What price are you placing on your social media activity? Are you calculating the cost of the staff paid to do it, or the social media agency who is acting on your behalf? Also, when thinking about your return, what are you measuring?

Are you measuring the impact through increased brand awareness or are you looking at directly generated sales? You will need to take a firm viewpoint and stick to it in order for your figures to mean anything period on period.

5. Calculating worth

You cannot attach a meaningful value to a social media fan or follower. Liking a page on Facebook is not the same as having the means to buy that brand. For example: you could be placing a meaningless monetary value on the Facebooker who "likes" your page yet spending zero money, while attaching no monetary value to the physical customer who actually buys your product without prompt from advertising or marketing.

This means that you can place an importance on a Facebook "like" when it has an actual monetary value of nil. For more on this read how Bulmers calculate the value of a fan on page 36.

Want to measure?

Having got this far, we can establish that your organization is open for business regarding social media and they understand you can measure social, but the question remains, do you want to measure?

1. What if my ROI is negative, I will look like a fool

Some people think measuring things is a punishment, as if they are not trusted to do what is always the most sensible thing. What if the answer that comes out the other side isn't what you expected? Maybe you are only getting a marginal positive return, if any at all. In this case it might be tempting to pursue the "can't measure" line of discussion, but don't give up. If you find out that something isn't working instead appreciate the opportunity to figure out why it's not working and improve it. Finding out you're doing the wrong thing is better than continuing doing that thing; it gives you a chance to focus on the strengths and address the weaknesses.

2. It's going to be too expensive to measure

As we will discuss further into the book there are some very good free tools on the market that can be used as a first step to cutting measuring costs. If the cost of measuring exceeds the cost of the return you have to ask yourself two things: a) are we making enough of a return to justify this activity? Or, b) are our costs for measuring the return too high? If the answer is yes to either of these two you should arguably not carry on with the activity without making changes, as you can't prove it's worth your investment.

3. Make decisions based on data

Over the years I've found myself in numerous discussions with people defending their gut instinct to pursue one business option over another and I've let myself be pulled into that kind of reasoning too many times. If you're up against a more senior team member you will always lose those debates. I've learned to reference data more, it's objective nature puts an end to the gut instinct line of reasoning. "Let's do a trial and let the data inform this discussion." It's the ultimate punch line.

In the end, you look pretty stupid when asked to defend a business decision that went wrong when it was driven by someone's gut instinct. Defending the same business decision based on data is a lot more comfortable, "the data suggested that . . .". You can't argue with data. You only need to make sure you have the right kind of data and the right amount.

4. Get the organization focused on what matters

Unless you're a fan of micromanagement, clear goals are essential to empower your peers to think for themselves and decide what would make the most sense in any situation they are faced with to take immediate action. When you provide them with updates on progress make sure the report focuses on actionable insight, this also includes findings about your competitors activities in the same space.

5. Benchmark

By going through the motions of setting up a scorecard to measure your activities, you get a benchmark to springboard from and the following year you can show how much you have improved the results. This would not be possible without the first assessment. This means that deciding and testing the variables you're benchmarking your activities against, will be more time consuming than the on-going reporting of results. Creating a base line gives you the opportunity to realistically develop targets that can let you under-promise but over-deliver.

Create your benchmark

To create a benchmark for your coming activities you want to start with an audit. If you are unable to do all the work yourself, or want to anchor this with more stakeholders in your organization, this is an excellent opportunity to organize a social media team, or a centre of excellence, with whom you can share the work. I've discussed audits and centres of excellence in the previous books so I will not go into any details here, but as a brief reminder:

The first activity is to define your **audience**:

- Who are you trying to reach?
- What does their journey look like?
- Where do you want to add touch points?
- What do they want to hear?
- What motivates them to buy your products?

The second activity is to **listen**:

- Where and how do you listen?
- Who influences your audience?

- What search terms do you want, and not want to monitor?
- How are your competitors stacking up?

Define goals

Once you have completed your audit you're in a position to start to define your goals. Depending on your business these will vary greatly but here are some common goals you might want to consider starting with.

1. Brand exposure

Eighty-nine per cent of respondents asked, stated that social media and marketing through social media had generated more business exposure. The addition of social media to multi-channel marketing campaigns brings with it increased opportunities to broadcast brand messaging and elevate brand awareness. This metric is not tied into direct sales or lead generation, but rather a holistic overview of brand and the heightened recognition that social media can generate.

Brand awareness may not be responsible for directly generating sales leads, but it is the gateway that customers pass through as part of a sales funnel. With increased exposure, it can be measured in terms of reach or how far your message is being broadcast across your audience. Increased reach will also raise the opportunities for you to engage with new followers and fans.

Through using social media analytics, companies are in a position to track brand awareness and begin to add a value to the activity.

By quantifying how campaigns are working, by measuring "likes", comments, retweets, pins etc., it then becomes possible to allocate future KPIs and so chart the rise of brand awareness through social media channels.

2. Improved customer relationships

In addition to the messages that you are broadcasting, social media allows you to converse with your customers and develop deeper relationships than those through more traditional channels.

This area is deep within the territory of intangible benefits as it looks at the value, interacting with your customers brings. To engage with your customers on a deeper level means that you can engage with them in a way which can stir or move them. This type of interaction will stay with the customer long after the conversation has ended.

By employing social media tools, which measure the online community for mentions of your brand, you are able to pick up on conversations which are already taking place. This offers the opportunity for your brand to jump in. This can be as important for the impact it can have on a positive conversation, as it can be for the difference your intervention can make on a negative conversation.

When thinking about how your message is viewed by users, a recent Nielson survey found that, on average, 92 per cent of individuals trusted the communications that they received from friends – and this is measured on a global basis.

3. Drive traffic to your website

It would follow that more digital activity would lead to more visitors to your website, but social media cannot be left to generate these without human input. There are key areas which will ensure that social media activity delivers the visitors companies need.

Using hashtags can bring more users to your site. Employed by both Twitter and Google+, you can leverage "trending" hashtags to increase traffic to your site. This is, in principle, like using a powerful advertising tagline as your own.

Blogging can be a very powerful way of directing people to your site by including links or longtails to improve your SEO. This can be reinforced by guest bloggers on other sites, linking back to you. You can also comment on someone else's blog and this can be used to drive traffic to your site.

Creating engaging content on a social media site can help drive traffic to your site by its quality and targeted nature. A good example of this is Pinterest. Pinning and Re-Pinning as many target images as possible and creating boards where you keep your own pins and then pins from others, means that you are able to increase the bandwidth of your influence and, as a consequence, develop your Pinterest authority. This means that your website links will become more visible and important on the Pinterest site, which means that there is an increased chance of user click-through.

4. Increasing market intelligence

Traditionally, market intelligence is the territory of the market researchers and the business analysts. When considering your digital market, you are now able to generate detailed analytic reports very quickly.

There are companies like HootSuite, Webtrends and Radian6, who will work with you to understand who and where your users are. They will also be able to assess the attitude and behaviour of your webusers, which will enable you as a brand, to understand how your customers are thinking about your brand.

Other methods of understanding what is happening as a result of your social media activity can come at no cost. These include LinkedIn Analytics, Facebook Insights and Google Analytics.

Google Analytics can be especially useful to track a customer journey through the webpage. You are able to understand where your users come from, i.e., the site they accessed yours from, how long they spend on the site and where they drop off. This can be important information when it comes to assessing the success of your business goals – for example, booking an appointment, requesting a quote or making a purchase.

5. Generate leads

This is the business end of social media and at the opposite end of the spectrum from increased brand awareness. While linking through posts, by using URL tools such as tinyURLs and bitly links, there are lead-generating opportunities which will generate leads.

Twitter chats are organized discussions that are hosted by a Twitter account. Specific hashtags are used to ensure that Twitter users will know when a new conversation is happening on the account, even though the subject of the chat can change. Twitter chat audiences are more focused as they have opted to be part of the conversation and, therefore, more engaged. When the chat is happening, you can position yourself as a source of knowledge and build friendly relationships with other users. You will also be able to follow them and track their future activities. This is like a warm sales lead that you can pick up in the future through direct messaging. This works most effectively if approached with a light touch.

LinkedIn allows you to access groups who operate in your areas of expertise. This is a lot like the networking which takes place in the physical world. Simply form a relationship by publically answering questions from those who need help. Give them a good idea of how you can help them, and follow-up with a more detailed response, using the Reply Privately feature.

What you think will work well in a given medium and what your consumers think, are two very different things. Like the CEO who only wants to use social media channels to push good news and thinks this will suffice, the assumption that consumers will consume any old data just because it's coming from your brand is false.

Before launching onto any social media platform, it's important that the first thing you properly evaluate is what information consumers want to receive, not what information you want to share.

Often, this information is not what you think. When newspapers first launched onto Twitter, the assumption was that consumers would follow newspapers to get a feed of shortened headlines and that would drive traffic through to newspaper websites. As it transpired users did not want feeds full of endless links. It was a lazy use of Twitter and an example of where businesses put their own objectives – driving traffic – above the needs of the consumer getting real time information. Things changed dramatically when journalists started using Twitter as a medium for breaking the news itself, rather than merely delivering out-of-date headlines. The message was changed to suit the medium and everyone benefited.

When evaluating your communications strategy put yourself in the consumer's shoes. Understand what they want to hear about. Hell – ask them! Then ensure you deliver it. In a world where the cost of set-up and delivery is the same no matter what size of business you have, if you don't give your consumers what they want, the chances are someone else will. This will not only affect your ROI – it will have a long-term impact on the survival of your business.

PS. Are you a member yet?

Don't forget the alumni network of fellow readers, people around the world that work professionally with social media. Join by searching for "The Social Media MBA Alumni" on LinkedIn. It's free of course.

2   Measure ROI by Platform

Learning Objective

In this chapter I will explain how you can use some of the build-in features in popular social media channels to track ROI. This is adequate for basic measuring to get you started.

Social media isn't limited to the websites such as those we have decided to feature here, social media in the broadest sense, is an opportunity to do business in a new way. It doesn't need to be customer facing, it doesn't need to be about getting people to buy something. However, sometimes starting out with getting your head around calculating the ROI for these channels can be an easy place to start. As you get the hang of it, you scale it to apply to all other social media-related processes in your business.

Facebook

Facebook states that they are the gateway to your customers. With over one billion people "liking" and leaving comments, on average, 3.2 billion times every day, they believe that their coverage will give your brand access to conversations taking place between friends, which will ultimately result in brand recommendation and become the start of the sales funnel.

What is the purpose of Facebook?

Facebook's origins are well documented, not least through the Hollywood film, *The Social Network*. Facebook came to life on the Harvard University campus in the US in 2004, when student, Mark Zuckerberg, launched the site to allow Harvard students to be as well-connected online as they were in real life. Facebook quickly filtered out to other Ivy League universities in the US before spreading across the world.

Facebook allows you to interact with your "Friends" as if you are interacting with them in real life. Facebook has evolved from an online meeting place to an online community with real advertising opportunities and brand awareness.

Getting started

Getting started on Facebook simply requires you to create a page, taking your own brand style into consideration. Once your page is created, you can begin to post. Posts are shown on Facebook's News Feed area which is where most people spend their time on Facebook, as they can see streams of their Friends' activity on one page.

Building an Audience is the second stage of the Facebook start-up process. Inviting a personal database, encouraging employees to "like" the page and advertising your Facebook page on your own website and printed collateral are typical entry points for new contacts.

Facebook advertising allows you to create paid-for adverts. Facebook states that people who have "liked" your Facebook page will spend an average of twice as much time as a customer, than people who are not connected to you on Facebook.

There are several advert formats which will deliver different outcomes:

Get More Page "likes": This gives you access to people who aren't connected to you yet. You are responsible for designing your advert.

Promote Page Posts: You can promote a particular post. This will increase your reach and your chance of being featured in the News Feed which will increase your adverts' "opportunity to see".

Get New Users: This ad will increase the number of people who will link to your Facebook app by targeting people who are more likely to install your app.

Increase Attendance: This allows you to increase the number of responses to a Facebook Event by targeting those most likely to join your event.

Advanced Options: Allows you to switch options with regards to how your ad is funded. This means that you can move between Cost Per Mille or impressions (CPM) and Cost Per Click (CPC). You can then set a budget and a time schedule for your campaign to run.

How can Facebook be measured?

Facebook offers an in-house service that allows you to hit your ad campaigns' targets in the following areas: Page "likes", Post Engagement, Page Engagement, App Installs, App Engagement, Mobile App Installs, Link Clicks (for offsite ads), Offer Claims, Event Responses and Conversions. They can create reports to demonstrate both how your ad is performing over your scheduled campaign and also report on the demographic of those engaging with your ad.

Facebook also offers Ad Level Reporting, which shows you a detailed breakdown of your total spend, a "cost per action", the breadth of your audience and the depth of their engagement with your ad, with a summary of targeting and performance. This is illustrated through a response graph which will track the performance of your campaign by clicks, click-through rate and impressions. This will allow you to understand not only what is happening, but also why it is happening with regards to content.

Content

Facebook is concerned with interesting visuals. Posts can be a combination of text, images or videos. Relevant content should keep people returning to your page – businesses often use Facebook to get customer opinion or feedback. Facebook suggests that you keep the content light, engaging and offer an alternative to a traditional corporate face.

The success of your content can be monitored using Page Insights. Page Insights will allow you to measure:

"Likes": Who "likes" your Page and how they found you.

Reach: The number of unique people who have seen your page content and their demographics.

Talking about this: The unique people who have interacted with your page by posting on your Page timeline, liking or commenting on your page or sharing your posts with their friends.

Performance metrics: The size and engagement of your audience.

Performance graph: How each post has influenced the number of people talking about your Page and your reach.

Page post insights: Analytics on each of your Page posts.

Facebook considers that when people interact with your page, they create a "story", which will go on to influence their friends and encourage growth within your brand.

There is an opportunity to create "sponsored stories", which are messages where friends encourage others to engage with your page. You can pay to promote these stories and therefore increase the opportunity to see these posts. Facebook's Ad Manager will help you measure your advert's performance. Ad Manager will monitor metrics from your advertising goals and your ad or sponsored story's cost per action and review your campaign summary graph to see how your content is performing and where it is not.

Costs

Budgeting for Facebook ads is interconnected with reach. Facebook will allow you access to an audience size, dependant on the parameters that you set, in terms of budget, and on the basis of demographics (gender, age, location) that you select. Facebook adverts are paid for on the basis of impressions, or CPM, or click-throughs, or CPC – if that is the option that you have selected in Advanced Options. Facebook will work within your budget as the ads will stop if you run out of credit.

How Bulmers calculated the value of a fan?

Bulmers is a cider brand owned by Heineken, the UK's leading producer of cider and beer, who have company headquarters in Edinburgh and London and a number of production sites across the country.

Their brand director is Michael Gillane and he has 15 years' experience within FMCG, starting his career at P&G and later at Premier Foods. He joined Heineken UK in January 2012 and manages the fastest-growing area of the business, the cider portfolio.

Bulmers is currently in the process of implementing a three-year social media strategy, the objectives of which are building share of voice, engagement rates and advocacy scores among cider drinkers in social. This social strategy also needs to be able to align and integrate with all brand communication and campaign activations as much as possible in order to establish exactly what the brand stands for in the consumer's mind: the start of great times with friends.

Market-leading research underpins their social media strategy. With the allocation of marketing budgets constantly a topic of boardroom discussion, being able to prove ROI had become increasingly important. So working with their social media agency, We Are Social, they set about demonstrating the benefit of investing in their Facebook community.

The agency and market researcher TNS developed an online panel survey to model the incremental value of a fan of Bulmers on Facebook versus a normal UK cider drinker. The survey asked questions about a range of cider brands, including Bulmers, and 241 fans of the Bulmers Facebook page completed it. This data was compared to a control sample of 198 general cider drinkers gathered by TNS, who answered the same set of questions.

The study showed that fans of the brand felt more favourably towards Bulmers versus the competition and, more importantly, consumed more of the brand than non-fans. Using this data, combined with the average retail value of their products, they calculated the weekly spend for both Bulmers' fans and the sample group. The statistics showed that Facebook fans were worth £3.82 more a week, or £200 per year; around 38 per cent more than the control sample.

The study wasn't limited to purchase behaviour. It showed that on average, 75 per cent of their fans were likely to share good brand experiences, promotions and discounts with their Facebook friends. It also gave them better insights into a range of behavioural questions, such as their consumers' attitudes towards different variants and flavours (Pear versus Original, for example), all more clearly put into context by comparing with the control panel.

Of course, there are some caveats to research like this. Facebook's EdgeRank algorithm will have exposed their survey to fans with a higher affinity to Bulmers and as interviews were done in a single day, it's unlikely the opinion of those irregular Facebook users who are Bulmers fans was captured.

It also doesn't distinguish between correlation and causation, but it does show that Bulmers' Facebook fans have a tangible value to the brand, and that the Facebook community is one worth investing in. In addition, defining fan value allows them to measure this over time and detect longer-term trends in the health of their online community.

Understanding the monetary value of Facebook fans enabled them to invest proportionately behind digital media. The insight gained from the research such as fans sharing good brand experiences resulted in the successful #BEGINWITHABULMERS campaign, engaging fans to share how they began their weekend with a Bulmers. This resulted in Bulmers becoming the most talked about cider brand on social media over summer 2013.

Twitter

According to Twitter, in September 2013, there were 400 million tweets a day and 200 million active users. Twitter, the microblogging site, exploded onto the social media landscape in 2006, capitalising on the burgeoning blogosphere.

What is the purpose of Twitter?

Twitter's definition is "a short burst of inconsequential information". In 2009, a market research company, Pear Analytics, based in San Antonio, USA, analysed 2,000 English-language tweets which came from the USA. This analysis took place over a two-week period in August 2009 from 11.00 am to 5.00 pm. They were able to categorize the tweets as follows: Pointless babble – 40 per cent, Conversational – 38 per cent, Pass-along value – 9 per cent, Self-promotion – 6 per cent, Spam – 4 per cent, News – 4 per cent. These figures demonstrate that Twitter was firmly ensconced in the personal territory of social media.

This comes in sharp contrast to what is sometimes referred to as "Twitter Revolutions", when Twitter is used to organize and galvanize support for protests, including the Arab Spring uprising of 2011, and the subsequent unrest that followed. During the Arab Spring uprising there was an increase of hashtags which mention the uprisings in Tunisia and Egypt. However, a study by the Dubai School of Government, found that the percentage of the respective populations active on Twitter was small: Egypt – 0.26 per cent, Tunisia – 0.1 per cent and Syria – 0.04 per cent.

Getting started

Twitter is a virtual network of interconnected relationships, whose growth relies on recommendations of connections and dissemination of information through sharing or retweeting posts. Twitter is also an online brand platform as companies and organizations can build their profile to reflect their brand personality. Twitter encourages new account holders to scope out what the competition are up to on Twitter before they issue their first tweet. They also encourage first-time tweeters to research what is already being said about them on Twitter. A count of mentions on Twitter is a basic metric which can be used to measure brand presence versus Twitter activity. This can also be measured to understand if non-Twitter campaign activity has an organic impact in the Twittersphere. That is to say, a user uses Twitter to comment on brand activity that they have viewed in a different digital or offline interaction.

How can Twitter be measured?

There are social media monitoring packages which allow companies to trawl the virtual world for mentions of their brand. These packages include Meltwater, BuzzFeed, TweetDeck, Buzzcapture, Brandwatch and HootSuite. Many companies use software packages like these to interact with users in an attempt to be perceived as excellent customer service providers or to "harness the negative" as they tackle customer complaints in the virtual world.

Twitter expresses success through popularity and numbers. Influential Twitter users are measured by their number of followers and tweets are "hashtagged" (#) by the user according to their content i.e., #worldcup, #skynews. "Trending" hashtags look at the most mentioned hashtags across the globe and success is yet again measured in basic statistics: who or what is trending, how often they trend.

Twitter themselves encourage brands to set their own metrics and to grow followers, promote retweets and increase coverage. Twitter also suggests you link your tweets back to your own site, thereby increasing traffic and conversions.

When drilling down to the finest of details with regards to metrics, Twitter has a two-pronged plan of action. The first is to analyse the content of your tweets and interact with your followers to access impact. This is a qualitative, rather than quantitative approach. The second, is too partner with one of Twitter's certified business service providers who will help deliver your metrics. Many of these companies also carry out Twittersphere monitoring.

The certified business partners are divided into three categories: Engagement, Analytics, Data. The Engagement partners can focus on reach, interactivity and content; Analytics partners can add values to these findings (they are often the same providers); Data partners will help you source existing networks and "piggyback" on existing activity.

Costs

Without taking the cost of partners into consideration, Twitter activity is free. There is, however, the option to boost your profile through paid Twitter activity:

- Promoting your account as quickly as possible is used to generate a critical mass of followers, including advocates and influencers.

This operates on the premise that an increased number of followers allows greater engagement and therefore greater opportunity for conversion.

- Using Twitter targeting to connect with users who have the same interests as your company or who are based in a certain geographical region or area.
- Listing your account in the "Who to follow" recommendation when setting up a new account or existing users.

Twitter only take payment when users choose to follow you. They also provide a real-time service to show how your influence has grown through a dashboard device. This will allow you to measure what your followers like in relation to your brand. This can also be broken down on a geographical or gender basis. This will allow you to inform market insight. You can also measure Twitter traffic to your site if you are using Google Analytics.

YouTube

What is the purpose of YouTube?

YouTube is a video-sharing website, which launched in 2005. Users of YouTube can upload, view and share videos which use Adobe Flash Video or HTML5. In the early days of YouTube, users would upload a combination of user-generated videos and vlogs (video blogs). They would also add clips from pre-existing TV or film collateral and share music videos. In 2006, Google bought YouTube as a subsidiary. Contributors have expanded it from the individual to the corporate, with selected media organizations such as CBS, BBC and VEVO becoming partners. This means that they show some of their own material via YouTube.

YouTube has had a huge impact on the music industry, with many artists launching new material exclusively on the site and the YouTube 100 is a weekly chart that notes the popularity of music videos. In 2013, the US chart, Billboard, began to include online streaming figures in its weekly charts. YouTube video users can impact upon the weekly music charts and this highlights the crossover between the virtual digital world and the real world.

According to YouTube, over one billion unique users visit YouTube every month and they watch over six billion hours of video. Over 70 per cent of YouTube traffic comes from outside the US. In March 2013, the Content Marketing Institute carried out a study looking at the YouTube videos of the Top 100 brands from Interbrand's 2012 *Best Global Brands*. They evaluated the impact of 200,000 corporate videos from 1,270 different YouTube channels.

They were able to demonstrate that over 50 per cent of videos from Interbrand's 2012 Top 100 had less than 1,000 views.

Why would you use YouTube?

Video content is the human face of social media marketing. It allows you to set mood and tone, to create an atmosphere and dynamism that is much more difficult to show on text-only social media sites.

You can post both video content to YouTube and embed YouTube videos in your own site. A linked relationship between a company site and YouTube can reinforce brand messaging across two online outlets instead of one. Using YouTube, as well as your own site, is important from the point of view of Search Engine Optimization. Through targeted SEO, you can ensure that searches rate both your own site and YouTube highly. This provides more opportunity for prospective customers to enter the mouth of your online sales lead funnel. YouTube will automatically ensure that your video content can be viewed across all multimedia platforms: PC, tablet, mobile phone.

YouTube True View advertisements are able to target users by giving an extremely informative breakdown of demographic information. YouTube will then also add a layer of behavioural and attitudinal targeting, which can choose a user audience that have been defined by the contextual circumstance, their geography, remarketing and their search behaviour. YouTube advertising is created to be shared, which increases reach and the opportunity for calls to action to be executed and sales leads to develop.

Getting started

Before creating your own YouTube Account, it pays to spend time on YouTube itself, browsing videos and seeing the type of content that the site hosts.

There are two ways to use your YouTube account. You can use it to select videos that you like or you can use it as a channel to broadcast your own company videos. Videos can be uploaded from a smart phone, tablet or computer. You can share your video widely or restrict its viewing to a controlled audience. Categorize your video by using keywords in the YouTube Tags section and name your video with a name that people can easily find.

YouTube is heavily focused on video content, and so the Help Guides often come in the form of videos: http://www.youtube.com/user/videotoolbox. They have a very firm sense of community and encourage users to behave responsibly on the site. The rules of the community should be read: http://www.youtube.com/t/community_guidelines. They also strongly advocate that their Brand Guidelines are read and adhered to.

How can YouTube be measured?

YouTube Analytics is headed by a dashboard which gives you an overview of your monthly activity. You can view visitor statistics and interactivity such as comments for example.

The Analytics also includes an Analytics Section, which documents the statistics surrounding your videos. These include number of views, demographics, where your site traffic came from, what devices your videos were watched on and how long the viewers stayed on your page. The last metric is called Audience Retention and it can show you several things about your video. A low Audience Retention figure suggests that the content of your video is not interesting enough for the user to stay with it to the end. It could also suggest it is overlong and requires too much commitment on the part of the user. It is important to look at the demographic breakdown of your audience, as the content could be very engaging, but merely targeting the wrong audience.

View Counter is the first metric which tells users a lot about your video. A low View Count for a recent upload won't work against the video – it's a recent addition and users will not expect many views. A video found through search with a low View Count can indicate that the video is targeting the wrong audience, as they haven't engaged with it in huge numbers. A very high View Count can indicate that a video is worth watching simply because of the high number of views that it has. This is viral territory, which can be defined when a video is shared beyond a user's second level of network connection.

Engagement reports give a level of qualitative data, focusing on the number of subscribers your channel has i.e., those who have made a conscious effort to align themselves with your channel. It will also detail likes, dislikes, number of people who have made it a favourite, comments and how widely your videos have been shared, all of which demonstrates reach.

LinkedIn

What is the purpose of LinkedIn?

LinkedIn claim that they are the conduit to the world's biggest professional audience. They connect professionals to one another and also to inspirational and influential leaders in the business world. LinkedIn connects 238 million professionals online, and while it emerged as a virtual professional network, it has diversified through the additional products and services it offers.

Why would you use LinkedIn?

Traditionally you would use LinkedIn to raise your personal professional profile. You can search for business contacts by name or LinkedIn can trawl through your email account contacts to see if there are any potential connections. Similarly, you can be invited to connect by someone else. It is advisable that you only connect with trusted acquaintances, but you are able to both filter or block invitations. You can easily remove a connection and LinkedIn don't inform the contact.

LinkedIn Corporate Solutions has been created to allow recruiters and headhunters to access the profiles that are created when a new member joins. The recruitment professionals will pay an annual subscription for access to these new members. This can cost tens or hundreds of thousands of US dollars. The new members are known as passive candidates – they already have a job and are not actively looking for a new position. LinkedIn has estimated that over two thirds of its members are professional recruiters.

Getting started

Your connections are ranked by degree of closeness. First degree contacts are direct. This means that you can email them directly, via LinkedIn. To contact second and third degree members you need LinkedIn services called introductions: InMail or OpenMail. You can operate on LinkedIn with a free account. This enables you to have limited access to the full remit of interconnectivity on LinkedIn. However, with a free account you are allowed five free introductions. Introductions only work if you have a direct contact in common with your desired contact and it is a two-step process to become LinkedIn. Also, either connection can decline to continue with the process.

You can bypass this convoluted system by upgrading to the Premium Service. Premium Service comes with an annual or monthly subscription and allows you to use InMail and OpenLink to connect. Both allow you to directly contact anyone on the LinkedIn network without the need for an introduction.

LinkedIn relies heavily on a need to know who is viewing your profile. You get to see a certain number with a free account, but a premium account means that you can see everyone who has viewed your profile. There are three premium accounts: Personal Plus, Business or Pro.

LinkedIn Groups mean that you can demonstrate to that part of the market you feel your company or organization operate in. In addition to sharing information and insights, you can display group icons in your profile which highlight your affiliation. There is a sponsorship option which enables companies to sponsor a group.

This allows companies and organizations to position themselves as business influencers.

LinkedIn Job Posts means that you can advertise your position to both active and passive candidates all over the world. You are able to see who is viewing your role and get a good understanding of their demographics. This can produce useful information for HR departments.

LinkedIn Talent Finder means that companies can seek out individuals who lie outside their networks which enables the targeting of passive and active candidates.

LinkedIn Ads allows you to place advertisements across the LinkedIn site. You simply select your target audience on the basis of their characteristics and LinkedIn displays your advertisement accordingly. The criteria you are able to set includes job title, industry, geography, age, gender, company size and company name. Set a budget and pay per click or per impression (number of times ad is shown). According to KISSmetrics, LinkedIn Ads deliver an average click-through rate (CTR) of 0.025 per cent. However, this can be boosted by targeting your ads as set out above.

LinkedIn Marketing Solutions has a unique ability to precisely target quality audiences in a business context, delivering high impact social media marketing solutions.

Company Pages is a central point where you can showcase the corporate side of your company news. This allows you to share developments with your products and services and highlight business opportunities.

Setting up your Company Page is straightforward. Visit: http://www.linkedin.com/company/add/show and add a company. LinkedIn encourages you to refine the content of your page. To do this, you click the "Edit" button on your Company Page to update your details and ensure that your content is Search Engine Optimized. Your first area for recruitment should always be your colleagues, staff and stakeholders, before driving your clients to your Company Pages.

You can add a "Follow" button to your website by taking code from developer.linkedin.com. This makes it easy for people to follow you on LinkedIn. You can use your Company Pages to engage and inform your customers and it is another opportunity for them to buy-in to your brand story. If your content is worth reading, according to your customers, they will recommend you to their connections and so your network of influence grows. Customers who "like" your Company Pages also have an option to Share them with their social media contacts by using the Share plugin. The Share plugin can be found at: developer.linkedin.com.

How can LinkedIn be measured?

Your LinkedIn Analytics page provides monthly metrics on your levels of engagement. You can measure the effectiveness of your Company Pages by using LinkedIn's analytics tools. The starting point is to measure the engagement rate. This takes the number of clicks, "likes", shares and comments, and compares them to the total number of impressions. This creates a simple equation to show that "x" amount of posting had a "y" rate of success. It means that you can tailor your content to be more demonstrably meaning-ful to your customers.

You can assess your amplification rate by measuring the ratio of "likes", shares and comments against the number of impressions. This will show what type of content your users like and how they share it with others.

Google+

Google+ is a recent addition to the social networking landscape. Google describe it as a "social layer" which enhances online connectivity. Google+ has over 350 million active users and between April and June 2013, it was used by 30 per cent of Smartphone users.

What is the purpose of Google+?

Google+ has created areas on a Google+ page which are named according to their functionality. These pages are templates which the user can customize when they register. The three main areas are:

- The Stream – the middle column on the page shows updates from connections in their Circles. The Stream allows you to post and add filters to show only posts from specific Circles.
- Circles – this is the creation of groups, organized on the basis of who you want to create a sharing community with. Other users can see a list of your Circles but not individuals' names. This is similar to the Friends function on Facebook, but how contacts are organized is a key differentiator. Circles also allows you to control the content of the Stream. Users are encouraged to label their Circles, e.g., family, friends, university etc. A "Following" Circle means that you can follow posts of people that you do not know personally.
- Hangouts – facilitates group video chats on the condition that the users have the Hangout's unique URL. Hangouts On-Air allows users to create instant webcasts on Google+. They can also be recorded.

Other functionalities includes "Messenger", (was Huddle) which allows instant messaging and photosharing within their Circles through their mobile devices; a "+1 button" for recommendations and "Data Liberation" which allows you to download your Google+ content. Google+ Communities allow users to start conversations about specific topics and allow the conversations to continue on an open-ended basis.

Google+ takes Google's experience and excellence in the search arena and marries it with personal information, preferences, likes and dislikes, to better inform both the user's search and social capabilities. This means that Google understands your customer as well as you do.

Getting started

First, create a Google+ profile or page. This is where your customers can find you so including all your relevant information is very important and specifically your website URL for easy navigation to your site. The next consideration is audience growth and content generation, which Google+ suggests are interdependent. They recommend frequent and fresh posting every three days in order to encourage a growth in followers. Following these steps will move your Google+ account closer to verification. Verification means that people who have received an email from you to their Gmail account will be given the option to link to your Google+ page.

The social annotations for the AdWords function allow people to see recommendations from your Google+ followers when you link your Google+ page to your AdWords campaign. Google+ claims that annotated ads receive on average of five to ten per cent more clicks. To maximize the benefits to your brand of Google+, you can connect your webpage to your Google+ page, using the Google+ badge. Google+ claim that top online publishers see, on average, a 38 per cent increase in followers after the addition of the Google+ badge to their site.

How can Google+ be measured?

Google+ has a service called Ripples. Ripples graphically demonstrates data to show you who is sharing your content with contacts and with what frequency. Ripples will allow you to identify influencers and the Circles that they influence.

Another key focus of measuring ROI on Google+ is the link with Google Analytics. Google Analytics can be manipulated to offer reporting that demonstrates how Google+ is impacting on your web traffic, inbound visitors and conversion statistics.

Costs

Google+ does not have any financial costs attached to its products, however Google Adwords campaigns come at a cost. These, in regard to Google+, must be considered in relation to the human and time resource required to keep content fresh, engaging and frequently changing.

Pinterest

Pinterest is a recent addition to our social media landscape, but it seems to have made an impact. According to Gigya's numbers in summer 2013, Pinterest generates 41 per cent of e-commerce traffic, compared to Facebook's 37 per cent. Brandignity state that Pinterest can claim "over 4 million daily unique users".

What is the purpose of Pinterest?

Pinterest was launched publically in March 2011 and has steadily gained momentum. Pinterest works by linking networks and boards and allowing users to understand what each other likes. In business terms, this allows you to build a picture of the behaviours and attitudes of your target market sectors. You can begin to piece together what your customers look at and invest a "click" in without using any budget on focus groups or quantitative surveys. The only Pinterest cost to a business comes through human resource and imagery.

Pinterest operates in the same arena as word-of-mouth, but in a virtual format. Like Twitter, the more active the pinners that pin your product and the more boards they pin on, the more influential they are in the Pinterest community. This can generate heat around your product and raise your online profile. In typical advertising terms, a high level of pinning is like increasing the "opportunity to see" or creating a virtual footfall which drives consumers to your online site through an organic-type search. It is feasible to gain interest for your product or service on Pinterest without having to use any advertising spend.

Creating an account on Pinterest is free-of-charge and adding the Pinterest icon to your own site involves the small act of cutting and pasting a little bit of code. When thinking about measuring the return on investment, it seems that adding Pinterest to your social media armoury comes with little monetary cost attached.

Pinterest requires high-quality, but small in size, images. They should directly focus on the product or service, or your output on Pinterest can become confusing for your audience. Like reading around an academic subject, you can start to add the option for pinners to choose images that are only indirectly connected with your product or service. By doing this, you can measure two aspects which are critical when building brand awareness:

- What do my consumers like and what don't they like? Are there any trends?
- To what degree are they interacting with my product? What "give" do we have in our brand? Can we make them pin things because our brand has?

Although many individuals use Pinterest as an online information sharing community only, there is an option to take your pins further by making them "rich pins". These pins contain images and information about what you have to offer. The only criteria you need to fulfil to create what begins to look and feel like little adverts, is to register with business.pinterest.com

Pinterest enables you to track and analyse traffic to your site from the Pinterest site with Pinterest Analytics. This free-to-use tool allows you to understand who is pinning your product or brand and where they are pinning you. Pinterest Analytics, like Google Analytics, means that you can develop a strategy that will allow you to test, adapt and refine the content and focus of your pins and track them throughout the day. This will allow short, sharp campaigns which react to a sudden need as well as build longer, slower-growing plans of activity.

As with many online communities, the impetus to get involved lies with the user – so it has to be as straightforward as possible to link from your product to Pinterest. This can include a Pinterest icon link from your website to Pinterest, but you can also encourage a link through email communications and even physically through labelling or in-store. This means that you can generate online interest from communications and opportunities that already exist.

When signing up to Pinterest, it's important to consider how online communities function. They work best if you get involved with the ethos of sharing. It is as important to "like" as to be liked. The cost implication for pinning other individuals or businesses is negligible – it really is the click of a button.

In order to grow your brand presence on Pinterest, it is worth considering a content strategy. The more pins you have and the more opportunity that you give consumers to pin, the greater the opportunity for your product to generate interest on the Pinterest community.

Blogs

For the purpose of this analysis, two mainstream blogs will be the focus: Tumblr and WordPress. However, data has been collected from sources which are considering a wider bandwidth of blogs.

A blog, which is short for web log, is a webpage that is an online journal or column that is accessed by web users. They err towards being shorter in length than magazine features and are updated frequently.

Blogs serve many different purposes and have evolved greatly since 2000, when they really entered common consciousness. Ranging from personal discourse to cutting-edge commercial content to political propaganda, blogs cover the full spectrum of content and tone.

Why would you use blogs?

Blogs can bring customers to your website through embedded links in the text. Blogs can be targeted at different audiences through targeting content. Engaging content can also bring customers returning to your site.

Search engine optimization and blogging work in close synergy to drive traffic to your website. Blogs are prose-style posts, which can easily contain longtail phrases which visitors use in real life.

When you are delivering constantly excellent content, you can stake your claim as the industry expert or the authority voice. This is an opportunity to stand out in the market where less-digitally focused competition is not in operation.

When you are posting a blog, you become your own publisher. This means that your company can highlight special offers or raise areas which are taking a sales dip.

Getting started

Tumblr

Sign up for your account at https://www.tumblr.com/register

You can now create tailor-made content on your Tumblr account through either posting blogs out or using Tumblr as a space where you can answer questions and queries. To create your post, simply write your text, upload images, testimonials, interviews, links, informal conversations, audio (embed tracks from Spotify, SoundCloud or an MP3), video (via YouTube, Vimeo or your own.).

Reblog on Tumblr. This is one of the key methods of sharing and generating reach on Tumblr. Select blogs to follow and find interesting posts to reblog. You can even engage with your customers and get them to send you their posts. This allows you to act like a broadcaster. Enabling "Asks" means that you allow questions from your followers and get market insight on your brands. You can publish your responses or direct message your customer.

When you have generated enough content, you can manage it all through Tumblr and use it to push your content out to your other social media channels, like Facebook and Twitter. You can also post to Tumblr from image and video sites, such as Flickr and Vimeo.

Like other social media sites, the more you interact with the community the greater your results can be. Liking, reblogging, following and tagging allow you to grow your influence in the Tumblr community. You can customize your Tumblr blog and Tumblr encourage it. They suggest that you contact creative designers and artists from the Tumblr community to help make your blog beautiful.

Advertising comes in the form of Sponsored Posts. These posts give you exposure via the Tumblr dashboard, where millions of people, Tumblr claim, will have the opportunity to see. A Sponsored Mobile Post means that mobile users will only see your post as they access the dashboard. Radar is Tumblr's flagship position on their dashboard and it can be exclusively sponsored by companies for maximum exposure on Tumblr.

Tumblr has its own Analytics tool that is accessed through the dashboard. You can measure reach and impact and compare your performance with competitor blogs.

WordPress
WordPress has a two-step start-up process.

1. Find a web host that supports WordPress. WordPress do state that there are many to choose from, but they do recommend Bluehost, DreamHost and Laughing Squid. You can also get a free account on WordPress.com.
2. Follow WordPress's five-minute installation. They have a comprehensive guide to help you do this, but they do stress it is very straightforward.

How can blogs be measured?

Although many blogging sites are free and it does not cost to host blogging space on your own site, blogging is a resource-heavy activity.

Calculating how much your blog will cost can be done. Use the following equation:

- Staff hours required per week to write, edit, track, manage the blog x salary per hour of the staff = weekly cost of staffing blog. This can be calculated on a monthly and annual basis too.
- Calculate the costs of overheads and benefits attached to that figure.
- Add any design costs, internal or otherwise, and calculate it on a weekly/monthly/annual basis as required.
- = Total cost of blog

How much does your blog generate?

How many leads does your blog generate? This includes phone calls, sign up, subscribing, quote request etc.

You can use your analytic tools to identify qualifying leads from your blog i.e., on the basis of time spent or frequency of visit. With personal communication you may also want to ask their point of entry.

What is the value of each lead?

- Calculate the revenue of the customer spend on the basis of an immediate spend, an eventual spend or a lifetime spend.

The formula to work out your blogging ROI is:

$$[\text{Revenue} - \text{blogging costs}]/\text{blogging costs} = \text{ROI}$$

PS. Are you a member yet?

Don't forget the alumni network of fellow readers, people around the world that work professionally with social media. Join by searching for "The Social Media MBA Alumni" on LinkedIn. It's free of course.

3　Tools

Learning Objective

From the previous chapter you will have gathered ideas to measure the ROI on individual platforms. If you want a holistic overview there are several tools that will help you.

In this chapter I will look at some of the most common tools used to monitor your performance against the goals you defined from the Strategy chapter. The selection here is based on those I have come across the most often; there are, of course, a wide range of options on the market. For that reason, I've also included some advice on how you make sure you get the most out of your supplier, whichever one you decide to use. The chapter also features a case study illustrating how to calculate the ROI from investing in a paid-for monitoring platform.

This chapter is for those of you not already using a monitoring tool or for those interested in sourcing a more sophisticated tool.

Choosing a supplier

Five ways to choose the best supplier for you and how to get the most from them

There are many social media suppliers to choose from and the market is also in a constant state of flux. With so much growth in this area, it can be tricky to keep abreast of the latest developments. The starting point for choosing your supplier, therefore, must be your objectives.

1. Objectives

You need to pinpoint exactly what it is that you need to do:

- Are you trying to assess your brand performance against the competition?
- Do you want to monitor the online chatter which is taking place in and around your brand?
- Are you hoping to assess movers, shakers and influencers in your industry and understand how the corporate face of your organization is working online?

2. Data requirements

What information do you hope to acquire from your analytics? And what depth of sentiment do you require?

- When you are looking for a geographical breakdown, are you working on the basis of understanding what country users come from and what region/state/county, or do you want to access the town/city level of data?
- If you are using analytics to look at incoming international traffic, will you need to translate any of the generated data?
- Will your company or organization want to drill down into the demographics of your website traffic?
- How exact do you need this information to be? Does it need to be specific, tracking each and every customer journey through

your site? Or are you trying to understand the ebb and flow of your online customers?

3. Resourcing

How will you deal with the data requirement and generation on a personnel level?

- Do you need instant access to the analytics tool to manipulate data for short-notice management reports?
- Will you want to manage the process in-house or have it managed for you by an agency?
- Will the channel be managed by an individual, a team within one department, on a matrix basis or as a hybrid between in-house and agency handling?
- How often will you want to maintain the reports? Are they static in order to generate constant like-for-like data or is it more important to probe bespoke areas and drill down to the minute detail.
- How does your brand name stack up with your competitors? Are they a world apart or are they close in meaning and spelling? (This is important in terms of the filtering required.) Is your in-house industry knowledge greater than any external agency can provide?

4. Costs

- How much have you got to spend – is it a basic package or is it a fully-functioning end-to-end service?
- How much time do you have to allocate against this activity? Will it be better to spend financial resource by outsourcing or will you benefit from meeting the time requirements in-house?

5. Longevity and experience

Although this is an emerging market in comparison to some more traditional forms of marketing, many companies have been around for a couple of decades. They have been around since the birth of web analytics and have created the shape of how many things operate.

There are also trendy little agencies that have been set up by digital natives. These are the people who have been born after the creation of the digital world. They can offer the bigger, more established companies a run for their money but may take a less traditional approach to business. You must find which type of company will work best with yours.

When you have chosen your analytics provider, it is important to remember that this is the starting point of your analytic analysis journey. The provider that you have chosen will offer different levels of service depending on your package.

There are several things you can do to make sure that you are getting the best value for money from your supplier.

1. Make your account manager work hard for you

There are many levels of support that your provider can offer. Some providers develop online training resources and communities. Other providers offer a high-level service, which means that the provider will take complete care of all analytics and deliver reporting. This option is available, but it may come at a cost. Google Analytics offers Google Analytics Premium, which will deliver all data and service required across the year for a flat fee of $150,000 (USD).

2. Take the time to watch the online seminars and webinars

YouTube corner the market in visual online support. Their help, https://support.google.com/youtube/?hl=en#topic=2676319, will take you through developing your videos to be engaging. The support on offer extends to optimizing your videos for mobile performance, the Partner Programme and Policies and Security. YouTube include a section on copyright and rights management.

3. Find your feet in their online community

Webtrends offers support across the spectrum, including helping users to find their own support network through talking with other Webtrends users. The Developer Network focuses on the technology end of the software. You can meet virtually with other users to troubleshoot data integration or migration. There is also a FAQ section where you can post your question and community members will answer it for you.

4. Undertake some online training

There are some very valuable training resources online which many providers offer as part and parcel of their website. These offer an overview of the product, yet can also tap into the key unique selling points of each product.

5. Plan some training

As well as providing a series of online webinars and training sessions that you can undertake at your own speed, Radian6 will come to your company and deliver training to you. They offer a tailored training session to best fit your need.

Popular measuring platforms

Google Analytics

What is the purpose of Google Analytics?

Google Analytics is a service which Google provides on both a free and paid-for basis. Delivering information and statistics on your website's traffic, Google Analytics can tell you where your visitor came from and what they did on your site. Google Analytics is targeted at marketers instead of the traditional web developers, allowing them to track critical market insight and metrics.

Why would you use Google Analytics?

Google Analytics enables you to watch your customer journey through your website, from entry to resolution. The data generated means that you can demonstrate your website conversions as a figure and with historical data, identify trends and develop a sales funnel which is invaluable in campaign marketing.

Google Analytics also means that you can see what your customers are doing on your site – where they linger and where and when they leave. This information is important to content marketers.

In Spring 2013, Google Analytics introduced real-time reporting, where you can watch your customers interact with your website live. In addition to watching customers, you can also get a Cost Analysis which details how effective leads are from your paid searches, social media channels, affiliates and organic search traffic.

Google Analytics have partnered with Google Display Network to provide you with the ability to find customers who have viewed your products or services. With this information, you are then able to target them as they search other sites and remarket to them.

Organic searching is increasingly important, with results being delivered by carefully considered Search Engine Optimization. Google Analytics SEO reports show clearly which Google Search queries brought users to your site.

Dashboards

You can access data via a Google Dashboard. The Dashboard collates data in one central place making navigating the information easy. You can create secondary dashboards for more specific information.

Google Analytics has many tools within its armoury. They include:

Flow visualization: Graphic representation of the users' journey through your site from entry to exit.

Map overlay: Analyses visitor data by continent, country and city and displays it on a map for ease of use.

Mobile traffic: Measures the impact of your mobile site or applications so that you can ensure they are working to optimum effect.

Social reports: Tracks the impact of your social media alongside your web activity to deliver an overview of the performance of your digital data.

Traffic sources: Allows you to understand where your site traffic is coming from. Google Analytics breaks this down by referrals, direct traffic, organic keyword searches and custom campaigns.

E-commerce reporting: Enables you to identify your key sellers if you are a product-based business. You will see what sells and the number of steps it takes to make a purchase.

Goal flow: Google talks about your business objectives in terms of "goals". Your goal flow demonstrates the customers' journey through your site from entry to objective – whether that be a purchase or an action. Goal Flow will also show you if and where they get stuck and where they leave. This allows you to make any necessary adjustments to your site.

Google uses Analytics in conjunction with its other products which, they say, will make your web presence more effective:

AdSense: If you allow third party relevant ads to be placed on your site, Google Analytics can include AdSense to understand where to display ads on your site to best effect.

AdWords: Google Analytics can import your AdWords data to show your visitors' journey after the point that they click on your ad. Google AdWords is a paid-for service. The integration with Analytics will enable you to interpret the effectiveness of your AdWord campaign.

Getting started

Set up your account

This is the first step in the process. In setting up your account, you will be given a unique identifier which you add to your site. Only you can access information about your site and you will need to set permissions to allow colleagues access.

If you already have a Google account, you can use you Gmail address and password to sign in. If not, you will be taken through the steps of creating one.

Next, you will need to provide Google with your site's URL. Name your account clearly. This will be useful if you come to add subsequent sites.

Select which country best suits your needs. This could be the country the site is based in or the country that it is servicing. You will also set the most appropriate time zone. After you add your details and agree to the terms of service, you will be given some code which you copy and insert into your website.

Insert Google Analytics JavaScript into your pages

In the last step, Google provided some code. You must include this code on every page that you want to be tracked. For most sites, it is a case of inserting the code into the HTML of your page and templates. Other sites may have different ways of doing this, but they should have bespoke instructions.

Once you have uploaded the pages back to your site, you can begin tracking information, although it may take a 24-hour cycle to collect something to analyse.

Get an overview of your site performance

Go to Website Profiles and click on View Reports to take you to your Dashboard. The top of the page is given over to a graphic showing your site traffic across the past month. This will only be possible from the time that you insert the code. Change the timespan to enable you to drill down to specific periods of time or click Compare to Past to compare two sets of data.

Visits, page views, pages per visit, average time on site, bounce rate, or percentage of new visits. The bounce rate is the percentage of people who leave your site.

See how your site is performing daily and hourly

If you want to understand the ebb and flow of traffic to your site you can do this using the Visitors functionality. You can view Hourly data to show how your site is performing at certain times of the day.

See where your traffic comes from

Below the main graphic on your Dashboard, you will see your site's top five most-accessed pages. You can click on these, then click on Landing Page Optimization and Entrance Sources to access a table of visitor sources, page views, unique page views (non-returning visitors), Time on Page, Bounce Rate and % Exit.

Frequent use of Google Analytics will increase your understanding and usability.

HootSuite

How to measure ROI on HootSuite

What is the purpose of HootSuite?

HootSuite is a social media dashboard that allows companies and organizations to create a central point from which multi-platform marketing campaigns can be launched across multiple social networks. Both individuals and teams can access and use HootSuite as they identify and grow their audience.

Why would you use HootSuite?

Via HootSuite, you can manage your brand across Twitter, Facebook, LinkedIn, Google+, Foursquare, Myspace, WordPress blogs, Vimeo, VIA.me, Reddit, StumbleUpon, Instagram, edocr, Tumblr, Evernote, Flickr, Get Satisfaction, MailChimp and SlideShare. There is also the functionality to add multiple channels to both monitor and post simultaneously. HootSuite is one of only a few partners who have been given full access to Google Plus's page application programming interface (API), and therefore access across the Google+ channel.

When thinking about Twitter and accessing Twitter, only 64 per cent of Twitter access is through the web page, Twitter.com. Sixteen per cent of Twitter use is mobile while 10 per cent comes from dashboards including HootSuite and TweetDeck.

HootSuite means that you can iron out any issues that you may encounter when more than one person is responsible for the upkeep of the social media accounts. Tasks can be delegated through Hoot-Suite and an audit trail created for reference.

As well as being able to communicate directly with your customers in real time, HootSuite allows you to store responses to frequently recurring and straightforward questions.

Another key function of HootSuite is the ability to work across platforms as it is a web app. Accessible from Mac OSX, Windows and Linux, HootSuite also works on iPhone, iPad, Android and Blackberry.

HootSuite delivers a free weekly analytics report by email, with a PDF showing: number of clicks per day, geographical information on the click-throughs, top referrers and most popular links. The report only tracks activity through HootSuite's own URL shortener, ow.ly.

Getting started

Sign up for your basic free HootSuite plan at https://HootSuite.com, or trial a paid-for plan. You can also register for HootSuite Mobile, which will allow you to access HootSuite when you are away from the office.

Begin to add your social networks to your HootSuite account. This means that you can begin to track and trace tweets and updates, monitor for brand mentions and begin to understand your social media traffic. You can organize your management of social media monitoring by using Tabs and Streams:

Tabs: Allows you to group streams and bring order to your dashboard.

Streams: Allows you to choose which information you are shown e.g. Home Feed, Updates.

You are now at the stage where your account is able to compose and send messages.

Installing Apps: The App Directory allows you to add third-party apps to your dashboard. These include Flickr, YouTube, Tumblr and MailChimp and may come at a cost.

How can HootSuite be measured?

HootSuite specializes in social media campaigning measurement, offering powerful analytics tools and reporting structures that you can customize. This software will enable you to put measurements in place across your social media outlets. Main reporting includes:

Facebook Insights: Understand your Facebook fans' "likes", comments and page activity on the basis of their demographic, region, language, and where they post from. Facebook Insights allow you to measure your reach, level of engagement, trending capacities and virality, set against a timeline. Historical data mean that you can scrutinize for patterns and trends.

Google Analytics: By employing Google Analytics and URL parameters, you are able to track web conversions back through their journey to the social media output. Metrics demonstrated include site traffic data, source, region, page views and bounce rates.

Twitter profile stats: HootSuite can provide an overview of your Twitter activity by highlighting number of followers and who they are following, allowing you to understand sentiment of posts and giving an indication of how your keywords are performing.

Ow.ly click stats: The first step is to choose individual or aggregated click stats for your shortened ow.ly URLs. You will then be able to produce data which considers region and date and will show referring sites and popular links.

Google+ Page Analytics: Google+ Page Analytics can also be accessed by HootSuite. This allows larger users to take measurements on a daily basis including daily growth, number of users added to circles, +1 shares, and posts per day.

Organization Analytics: Organization Analytics can be used to analyse the work of your social media team to better understand the metrics involved. This allows you to trace the lifecycle of the post or query through your internal organization, from origin to resolution.

Analytics Reports: HootSuite Analytics Reports are updates that can be shared across any HootSuite user.

Radian6

How to measure ROI on Radian6

What is the purpose of Radian6?

Radian6 is a platform that allows organizations and companies to scan the internet for conversations and interactions which are taking place in the social space. Radian6 is able to identify and monitor sources and report its findings through a series of dashboards and graphic devices. The platform monitors news streams, blogs, forums, comment areas, photo and video sharing sites, such as Flickr and YouTube, Twitter and Facebook.

You can then choose from separate elements to create bespoke reporting on the searches that you created:

- **Analysis Dashboard:** This real-time platform allows you to monitor and engage with conversations based on your search criteria.
- **Summary Dashboard:** A pre-defined application which allows you to understand the volume of the conversations you are looking at. The summary dashboard will also track the general feeling of the conversation, show you key demographics involved and high-light who the influencers are and what they are saying.

- **Insights:** Radian6 combine their data with that of third-party partners. This allows you to dig deeper behind each post to create a picture of the author. Insights shows gender, age group, their geography and interests. It also uses this information to create lists about what is being most talked about and the feelings towards the subject area.
- **Radian6 MobileApp:** The Radian6 Mobile App allows you to keep abreast of conversations even when on the move. You can either interact directly or forward it to another colleague to deal with it.
- **Engagement Console:** The Engagement Console provides a platform for coordinating your activity and interactivity. You can also access your Twitter and Facebook accounts through the Engagement Console.

TopTenREVIEWS awarded Radian6 a silver award in 2013, stating that using this platform is "exhilarating". TopTenREVIEWS continues to praise Radian6 for its minimal user input to achieve solid and robust data that can be manipulated in many ways to deliver meaningful results to show how your social media is performing.

Why would you use Radian6?

Radian6 can be used across your social media monitoring. You can also employ Radian6 to understand how your campaign and its messaging are being understood by the audience and how they are performing. You can:

- **Track and monitor your messaging:** Track the spread of your news releases and communications in terms of bandwidth and speed in real time. You can follow where your messaging goes and how it is used by online users. This will give you the ability to identify key influencers and form a relationship with them.

- **Identify sales opportunities:** You can recognize potential sales opportunities through access to the content of users' messages. This will allow you to hone in on events, issues and concerns and take control of the situation.
- **Measure yourself against your competitors:** Track your competitors at the same time as you track yourself for a useful comparison.
- **Appreciate what's trending in your industry:** Follow, understand and forecast what has and is being said in your marketplace. This will also allow you to consider forecasting future trends and prepare accordingly.
- **Crisis management:** Harness any negative sentiment or publicity from the outset. This allows you to retain control and exercise damage limitation.

Getting started

The fundamental principle of Radian6 is the Topic Profile. Your Topic Profile is a bespoke set of keywords about your company or organization. You can target these keywords, taking language, media and geography into account.

By constantly monitoring your keywords, your output will be much more effective. However, there are basics you need to cover:

- Your brand or product name.
- How it could be used by your customers, including any room for erroneous spelling.

- Your Twitter handle, if you have one.
- The types of information you are looking for – product issues, potential customers, comparison processes etc. Radian6 have a list of Trigger words that might help.
- Consider what language people use to communicate on social media and mirror it in your keywords.
- Create groups of keywords for ease of monitoring.

You can also attend an online Radian6 keyword session to get you up and running.

How can Radian6 be measured?

To recap, Radian6 will measure online buzz about your company and organization based on the keywords that you submit to them.

David Alston, CMO of Radian6, is at great pains to point out that Radian6 does not deliver data that can be traced through the revenue funnel. He does continue to say that this is a qualitative tool which can take the temperature and measure the buzz surrounding your brand.

Dashboard Overview

You can view the results of your searches through the Dashboard Overview and you can identify the best performing keywords. The results can be displayed in Conversation Clouds, which display the 50 most used terms linked with keywords. Graphically, this can be displayed in a bar chart or line chart.

The River of News facility allows you to display the following strands in relation to a specific keyword or topic: media source, level of influence and general feeling of the post.

This enables you to understand how your customers talk about you and your product. This could complement the output of traditional qualitative focus groups.

Engagement Console

The Radian6 Engagement Console means that you can interact with the posters. You can tag, highlight, add notes, respond and understand how your team is interacting with their wider audience. You can include multiple Twitter accounts, a Facebook account and multiple bitly accounts for fully integrated engagement.

You can also instigate the interactivity by sending messages out. Sending more than one message out at a time can be done through the use of Radian6 Stacks. This allows you to launch across your social media simultaneously.

Like the Analysis Dashboard, you are able to allocate work and tasks to the wider team via the Engagement Console.

Summary Dashboard

The Summary Dashboard explains your reporting using graphic-based visuals. One of the core elements is the Infocube. Infocube displays critical metrics about your brand including: overall performance, volume of buzz, notion of feeling, demographics, key influencers and post content.

There are many levels of user across the platform, ranging from the highest level of permission, to read-only. Access to your Radian6 account can also be shared by any agency you use to manage your social media output.

Webtrends

How to measure ROI on Webtrends

What is the purpose of Webtrends?

Webtrends is an American company who are one of the original leading forces behind web analytics and have been in operation since 1993. Webtrends's products and services break down website performance so that you can understand how your website is working. They are able to look at the user statistics of a website and treat it like the physical world of marketing. That is to say, they are able to apply structure to an audience. This includes customer intelligence and behavioural segmentation where website users are identified and classified according to what they do and how they do it. They also offer analytics across all digital platforms, including web, mobile and tablet access and social media. This allows you to understand how customers are interacting with you in the digital world.

Why would you use Webtrends?

TopTenREVIEWS has awarded Webtrends Analytics 9 their 2014 Bronze Award as it is one of the few web analytics providers who are 100 per cent compliant with the Web Analytics Association defined analytic terms. Through their digital platform, Webtrends focuses on collecting pieces of information that companies can manipulate to their advantage, and ensures that they stay ahead of their competitors. The majority of Webtrends products can be used as installable software or as an "on demand" product, which means you can tailor-make your solution. There is no free version of Webtrends available, but they do offer a free trial.

The level of reporting that you can generate with Webtrends can be specific to the hour. This can be helpful if you are analysing a launch performance or a crisis-management situation. The level of data gathered can be so targeted that it allows you to create hyper-targeted marketing campaigns.

Webtrend's Care Plan is available to buy, which means that you have access to customer support via telephone, email, knowledge base, and online chat support. Although there are no free Webtrends products, they do offer a series of guides to talk you through the essential nature of web analytics.

Webtrends have several products and services on offer. Webtrends Multi-Channel Measurement enables you to manage the user data you are receiving across your digital channel and analyse its impact through a dashboard. The dashboard data will mean that you can gain an overview of exactly how you find, engage and hold on to your customers. You will also be in a position to measure conversions and track user experiences through your site. Webtrends will create and develop a measurement strategy that will help you identify key areas of success or issues against your marketing strategy.

Heatmaps are a feature of the Multi-Channel Analytics. Heatmaps allow you to add a visual overlay to your pages which picks up where user activity is happening; that is to say where they are clicking or running their mouse over. Heatmaps can be used in real-time and will help you assess which areas of your site are converting your customers and which are not. The image generated shows hotspots of activity and darker spots of inactivity.

Webtrends Streams™ is a product that produces data on each individual site user. You are able to watch the user interact live with your site. This means that you are able to interact with your customer as they are transacting with you.

Webtrends also offers a product which focuses on internal communications. Webtrends Collaboration Optimization means that companies can collect data on company intranets and internal social networks to understand how employee collaboration is working. This enables internal employee-facing communications to be tailored more effectively, which results in greater impact on the ground.

Webtrends Social Measurement delivers measurement of the customer journey from the point of engagement on the social media forum to website conversion. Webtrends have a hands-on approach with this product as they will design and manage your social media measurement strategy on your behalf.

Webtrends Mobile Measurement means that you are able to drill down to the detail of the user's mobile behaviours. This will demonstrate the levels of customer usage of apps, social media via mobile and QR codes. This enables companies to engage with their customers on a more meaningful level via mobile phones, as behaviour can be accommodated and reacted to.

Getting started

Webtrends offers a bespoke and tailored service. To access any of their products, you must make contact with Webtrends. This can be done through their bases in Portland, Seattle and San Francisco in the US; Melbourne in Australia; Uppsala in Sweden or their office in London, Great Britain. Their website holds vast amounts of information about their products and they offer many resources to help you understand what product would work best for you and how it actually works. They also have extensive online support teams, who are on hand 24/7 to assist you.

Measuring the ROI on your choice of platform

Jeanette Gibson
Senior Director, Social & Digital
Marketing at Cisco
@jeanetteg

Background

In April 2012, the IT hardware maker, Cisco, undertook a broad evaluation of its social and digital marketing strategy and the results of its pilot with a range of tools, one of which was Radian6. They decided to establish a social media listening centre that could map, track, and manage social interactions.

Working with its PR agency, the Cisco team spent about three months building up its social listening strategy and putting the appropriate reports and dashboards in place. Cisco decided to use a hub-and-spoke model for its listening centre, with five core team members responsible for monitoring on an ongoing basis, ambas-

*Contains extracts from *Salesforce Radian6 case study – Cisco* (c) copyright salesforce. com, inc. Used with permission.

sadors within each business unit, and a network of subject matter experts that could engage with customers.

The centre now tracks ongoing and trending topics and sentiment, and can also be configured to support short-term listening goals such as a vertical or business unit launching a new product, Cisco's sponsorship of the summer Olympics, or its annual trade show, Cisco Live. Cisco's social listening playbook defines triage for different kinds of mentions, looks at the urgency of response needed and then routes the mention to the appropriate employee for action.

In the end, Cisco moved forward with Radian6. By creating a centralized and standardized strategy for managing the growing volume of social mentions it receives, the company now has a complete view of customers and uses those insights to identify leads, solve service issues, and improve overall engagement with its customers.

Today, Cisco's social media listening centre manages more than 5,000 mentions a day, supporting more than 70 company-related Facebook pages and 100 Twitter accounts.

Key benefits of the project include:

- **More focused use of outside creative agencies:** By standardizing and having one social listening centre that triages all of Cisco's social interactions, Cisco can ensure creative agency fees are invested in thought leadership and innovation in the social engagement space, rather than simply managing tweets.
- **Increased staff productivity:** Cisco's triage system, named ABCs (action-based conversations), and its ability to leverage a broad field of subject matter experts via mobile device access, enables its employees to respond to social mentions in a time-appropriate way from anywhere, thereby driving greater overall productivity.

Additionally, triage reduces the overall time needed to respond to mentions and reduces the number of customer interactions or questions that might ultimately result in a call to a support centre.

- **Increased customer insights:** Because Cisco can mine and analyse customer and partner social mentions in a meaningful way, they can have a better overall view of sentiment and behaviour that would be cost-prohibitive to achieve through traditional means such as surveys.
- **Increased profits:** Although Cisco's social listening centre is relatively new, insights gained from monitoring have already resulted in sales opportunities that might otherwise not have been recognized.
- **Improved partner management:** Cisco is expanding its use of their tool to support partners, as well as providing a more scalable and cost-effective way to keep partners engaged, other than traditional partner programmes.

Net Cash

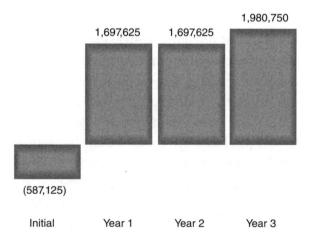

Figure 3.1: Net Cash Flows

The costs

Cost of the project includes software license subscription fees, outside creative agency and consulting fees, hardware, personnel, and training. The software license subscription fees represent the additional incremental license subscription investment Cisco made in standardizing on Radian6, which had previously been purchased on a one-off basis by different departments (along with other social monitoring solution subscriptions). The hardware investment Cisco made was for its Cisco Interactive Services Manager which includes touchscreen interactive displays for monitoring social trends.

Establishing a clear structure and triage system for how social mentions would be addressed and in what time frame, was critical to Cisco's ability to scale and manage its social listening centre. Not all social mentions warrant, or are best served, by an immediate reaction; Cisco's model enables it to ensure the interaction resulting from a social mention is context- and time-appropriate.

Cisco also recognized that social listening couldn't occur in one corner of the business.

Although the social listening centre is managed by a few employees, a broad team of part-time ambassadors are part of the overall social conversation. Cisco has also invested in kiosks and dashboards outside the centre (in the CEO's and CMO's offices, for example), so executives and others are aware of social trends and listening strategies on an ongoing basis.

Calculating the ROI

A third party consultancy quantified the initial and ongoing cost of software license subscription fees, hardware, consulting services, personnel, and training over a three-year period to calculate Cisco's total investment. The ROI calculated is based on the incremental additional investment and benefits Cisco achieved by standardizing their listening strategy.

Direct benefits quantified included the avoidance of additional creative agency fees and additional contact centre staff that would have been required to achieve the same result without standardizing the social listening centre, as well as avoidance of survey expenses. Indirect benefits quantified included the increase in productivity of those employees responsible for social engagement who can access the application via their mobile devices.

Not quantified were the increase in profits based on new sales driven by social media mentions, or the returns from expected increase in partner engagement and retention driven by extending the social listening reach to Cisco partners.

Result:

ROI: 281 per cent
Payback: five months
Average annual benefit: $1,596,292

PS. Are you a member yet?

Don't forget the alumni network of fellow readers, people around the world that work professionally with social media. Join by searching for "The Social Media MBA Alumni" on LinkedIn. It's free of course.

4 Case Studies

Learning Objective

You have now heard about the theories and how to develop an ROI strategy. You've seen some basic and more sophisticated ways of measuring ROI directly within social channels and via third-party tools. However, before you start doing it for yourself, here is some more inspiration from people that have already made the journey you're about to embark on.

In this chapter we are going to meet individuals responsible for the social media strategy at a range of different companies, different industries, customers, goals etc. They will outline their social media strategy and ROI methodology as well as share some hard-earned insight for your benefit so you don't make the same mistakes.

O$_2$ – customer service

About the company

O$_2$ is the commercial brand of Telefónica UK Limited and is a leading digital communications company. With over 23 million customers, O$_2$ runs 2G, 3G and 4G networks across the UK, as well as operating O$_2$ Wifi and owning half of Tesco Mobile. O$_2$ has over 450 retail stores and sponsors The O$_2$ Academy venues and the England rugby team. Read more about O$_2$ at www.o2.co.uk/news.

The interviewee

Kristian Lorenzon currently holds the position of Senior Social Media Manager at O$_2$ Telefónica UK, after spending the past few years of his career specializing in digital and social media planning for various UK and global brands. Kristian oversees O$_2$'s central social media strategy, governance and the delivery of commercial and customer engagement activities. Areas of particular interest include consumer responses to new media, and social media's role in omni-channel retailing.

@krislorenzon

Their social media strategy

O$_2$ coordinates company-wide activity through main company social media profiles. This gives the brand the ability to integrate social media campaigns with a centralized brand presence. All social media usage throughout the organization is governed by a single policy and a central team of social experts manage all social media activations. O_2 uses a hub-and-spoke business model to ensure there is a single source of governance and communication through social media. This model provides direct support and consultancy to the various business units within the organization, allowing for scalability as social media channels become an increasingly important and in-demand resource within the organization.

Over the past three years, the organization has developed a bespoke social listening and insights tool that gives business intelligence and the company's marketers invaluable information about its customers to inform campaigns and decision making e.g. interests, hobbies, desires, sentiment and likelihood to recommend.

Their journey to measuring ROI

O_2 decided to be active on social media in 2008 and like many brands there was no clear strategy; rather the objective was to test and learn on the fast-growing channels like Facebook, Twitter and YouTube. Conversation levels were a lot lower than they are now and there was no expectation for O_2 to be actively interacting with customers. People were talking about services and products (70 per cent), sponsorships (20 per cent) and product and network support (10 per cent).

The brand built goodwill by starting to do a certain degree of customer service on channels including forums and Twitter. At this stage, there were no set KPIs in place and no measures of commercial return on investment. The only measures in place were channel based including reach, interactions and clicks. These days, the brand can be found responding to customers on most online channels. Customer services now make up 80 per cent of all in-bound enquiries on social media; the remainder of mentions are campaign, brand and sponsorship related. This is where valuation becomes rather difficult. What's the value of not being able to respond to a customer in a crisis? How does that compare with mentions around a campaign?

What they measure

Tata Consulting Services (2013) suggest that almost two-thirds of big businesses have at least one full-time employee dedicated to using social media, but only 10 per cent are reporting benefits to the business resulting from the investments. These figures are astonishing, especially when you consider a brand like O_2 has around 30 people touching social media on a daily basis. These are large investments that need to be measured and to set KPIs. O_2 have three defined areas of social media measurement which are broken down into channel, campaign and commercial.

Channel measurement is arguably the easiest of the three. O_2 look at data points that include but are not limited to: Impressions, Visits, Followers, Mentions, Share of Voice, Sentiment and Clicks.

Campaign measurement is more bespoke and built around specific objectives surrounding each campaign that could include: Awareness, Referrals/Leads, Message Association, Brand Association, Change in Sentiment, Conversion, Favourability and Purchase Intent.

Commercial measurement is arguably the most important when reporting on overall performance, focus for business and return on investment. These include: Customer Satisfaction, Cost Savings and Revenue.

How they measure

There are many metrics in place to measure the effectiveness of social media communications at O_2. The most important and influential of these are commercial objectives including Customer Satisfaction (CSI), Cost Savings and Revenue.

Customer satisfaction and value

O_2 have linked CSI to customer value (profitability) so they can make the case for investment in customer experience across different customer touch points. To measure CSI, over 30,000 interviews are conducted annually. The CSI measure itself is based on three questions:

1. In general, how satisfied or dissatisfied are you with O_2?
2. How well does O_2 meet with your expectations?
3. Try to imagine a telecommunications company, perfect in all regards. How close or far from this ideal is O_2?

Drivers analysis is used to identify which touch points have the highest impact on overall satisfaction. Facebook, Twitter, YouTube and forums are included as part of this analysis to help O_2 understand how they are performing in specific areas.

Overall, as of October 2013, customers that interact with O_2 on social media have on average four points higher satisfaction versus other touch points. This means that customers interacting with O_2 on social media have a higher long-term value than others that don't.

Cost savings

On average, 5,000 customer service interactions occur each week on social media. This accounts for a significant cost saving for the business with more than 90 per cent of customer interactions on social media resulting in a deflection from call centres. This is measured on a monthly basis by looking at the cost of servicing customers on social media versus voice. The calculation is as follows:

> Number of unique customers serviced **times (×)**
>   percentage of those that reach a resolution **times (×)**
>   traditional handling cost (voice) = **cost avoided**
>
> **Minus (−)** cost of social media team = <u>net cost saving</u>

Revenue

O_2 use industry recognized social media and analytics platforms in order to understand the customer journey. Revenue through social media is measured on final click, i.e., after a customer engages with content across O_2 social media channels do they end up making a purchase on the O_2 online store.

Example

Customer response on social

There are up to 30 people within O_2 that touch social media on a daily basis, the large majority of these people are Community Managers and Customer Service Agents. All social media interactions come through one central monitoring and engagement tool that was purpose built for O_2 UK to manage large volumes of mentions, interactions and agents.

O_2 monitor all brand and product terms online and actively respond to customer enquiries across main social media platforms (Facebook, Twitter, YouTube and Google+) and forums. All mentions are screened by O_2's Community Managers who operate from 8.00 am to 10.00 pm daily. General brand chatter and "banter" is dealt with by front-line Community Managers who engage in meaningful conversation with customers. All customer service enquires including billing, tariff and upgrades are tagged and sent through to the relevant customer service agent to respond to the customer in private on the relevant social media channel. These interactions equate to an average of 5,000 per week, with an average voice deflection rate of 90 per cent on a channel that is more cost-effective to operate.

Lesson learned

Start with customer insight and measure what matters to customers. Customer satisfaction is the number one KPI at O_2, as happier customers stay longer and are more valuable to the brand. Channel and campaign measures are very important but it is important to understand the relationship between measures and the linkage to commercial objectives. Commercial value = commercial investment in channel.

Drive actionable insights and feedback into business from social media. Fully integrate social media through Business, Brand, Marketing and Sales/Service. Use social data to tell a story about the customer in order to drive positive change and improvements to products and services.

Sabre Hospitality Solutions – business development

About the company

Sabre Hospitality Solutions provides technology to the hospitality industry and advise their clients on how to make the most of social media. It operates one of the industry's largest Software-as-a-Service businesses, with its reservations and property management system, marketing and distribution software, and internet marketing and e-business solutions used by more than 18,000 hotel properties around the world. Each year, it generates more than $5.85 billion in revenue for its customers. Sabre Hospitality Solutions is part of Sabre Holdings, a global travel technology company serving the world's largest industry – travel and tourism. For more information please visit: www.sabrehospitality.com

Sabre Hospitality Solutions, @SabreHosp, works with clients in the hospitality space, developing and executing strategies to help their clients create successful social media marketing campaigns.

The interviewee

With a background in PR, Megan Peterson worked as Sabre's Social Media Specialist for almost four years before being promoted to their Social Media Manager, which is the position she currently holds.

@sabrehosp

Their social media strategy

They encourage a comprehensive social media plan that includes management of profiles to drive engagement as well as promotional campaigns to drive profile growth, brand visibility, and revenue generation.

Generally, Facebook and Twitter are the top two platforms that their clients use because of the ability of these networks to reach broad audiences and cater to businesses through tools such as advertising and integrated analytics. Depending on an individual business's needs, YouTube, Flickr, Instagram, Pinterest, Google+, Foursquare, and LinkedIn are also important networks to include in a hotel's social media strategy. The recent introduction of the ability to remarket to website visitors on Facebook was an especially important development as it opened up Facebook as a more prominent channel to drive revenue in the hospitality industry.

Their journey to measuring ROI

The strength of social media is that it provides access to reach users in the spaces they spend most of their time in order to build relationships with users and strengthen the brand. If a brand does not measure performance of its social media profiles, it risks losing visibility or even alienating users, which is in direct opposition to social media's goals of increasing brand visibility and building relationships. Brands have to measure the performance of profiles and advertising on social media channels in order to optimize content and campaigns.

What they measure

The company focuses primarily on Return on Engagement with social media activities, unless it is a campaign specifically designed to drive revenue. Return on Engagement refers to the idea that the effort a brand puts into managing a social media profile is being returned in the form of interactions from users.

A strong social media profile is measured in follower growth as well as steadily high levels of engagement, which includes "likes", comments, clicks, photo views, video views, retweets, and favourites. When users are interacting with a brand's content, it demonstrates an affinity for the brand which allows the brand to market to users. Since hotels are rarely an impulse purchase, building strong relationships with customers on and offline allows a hospitality company to drive revenue in the long run.

How they measure

There are countless social media analytics platforms available, but in terms of accuracy of data and usefulness of information, the company has found that the internal analytics platforms offered by social media networks, including Facebook Insights and Twitter Analytics, are the most reliable. In order to show the holistic performance of social media, they also uses Google Analytics data to see how users from social media networks are using the website and to ensure that any social media campaigns that are sending users to the website are performing strongly.

In addition, they also use internal analytics platforms to measure performance of advertising campaigns on social media. Social media ad campaigns often have different success metrics than traditional ad campaigns. Reporting is tailored to an individual campaign's goals, whether that includes revenue, follower growth, social media engagement, or website engagement. Reporting on social media should always be adapted to each campaign's goals.

Given the ever-changing face of social media, Sabre Hospitality Solutions re-evaluates its benchmarks annually to keep the measurements of success up-to-date and relevant to clients' evolving needs. In addition to helping define success for campaigns, studying trends in performance data for different types of campaigns and different types of properties helps Sabre Hospitality Solutions to identify which types of promotions are most successful and to develop more successful strategies tailored to their clients' issues.

Lessons learned

- **Don't get stuck in a rut:** social media is an ever-evolving field, and if you do not allow your strategies for execution and measurement to evolve, you will fall behind the pack.
- **Don't discount engagement:** revenue is important, but the greatest strength of social media is building relationships, and if you are not measuring engagement, you are not seeing the full picture.
- **Don't go with the flow:** just because a strategy works for one company does not mean it will work for you. Know what your needs are and what your goals are for your social media campaigns, and make sure you are measuring performance against those goals.

Makino – sales

About the company

Makino is a global manufacturer of machine tools that supports the automotive, aerospace, heavy equipment, medical and die/mould industries. In addition to machining equipment, the company supports manufacturers with software, engineering services, automation systems, training and capital financing. Its North American operations are supported by 550 employees.

The interviewee

Mark Rentschler has served within the manufacturing industry for more than 30 years. His career at Makino began in 1995 as the company's service parts manager and then later taking on the role of marketing manager in 2001. In this position, he has transitioned Makino's marketing efforts from traditional print-based media into award-winning digital marketing campaigns.

@makinomachine

Their social media strategy

In 2012, following years of stagnant or negative growth, the US witnessed a renaissance in manufacturing. This dramatic comeback created new opportunities within the machine tool industry to gain market share for Makino. The company capitalized on this economic environment by launching a new marketing campaign, "Make What Matters", with the goal of recognizing and supporting the manufacturing professionals who produce the high-quality components used in products that impact our daily lives. This inspirational narrative fuelled customer-centric content development, and it became the rallying cry for the company's social media programme.

Makino's strategy for the Make What Matters social media programme was to bring the campaign narrative to life through social engagements where audiences participated in discussions about how US manufacturers were making what matters for their companies, communities and industries. The backbone for this social strategy was Makino's extensive library of custom content, which included case studies, technical articles, white papers, webinars, imagery and videos. This content was adapted across Makino's Facebook, Twitter, LinkedIn, Google+ and YouTube communities to drive web traffic to compelling customer stories and inspire audience members to discuss their experiences with peers. This combined impact of audience insights and relevant content created a platform for Makino audiences to be heard.

Social media editorial calendars were prepared on a monthly basis to ensure a steady and continuous stream of new content, with each week strategically prepped to include engaging questions, customer stories, technical advice and industry news. Audiences were encouraged to upload photos of themselves with their Makino machines and share what they did to make what matters. Traditional, magazine-style case study articles were repurposed into smaller, more easily digestible content formats, such as video testimonials, infographics and "Story Albums", which used text-overlaid images to share customer stories and quotes.

The Makino team researched key customers and target accounts to discover their corporate social media properties. Those with a presence on social media were followed and monitored by Makino in order to share and promote success stories in the spirit of Make What Matters – an effort that led to reciprocated follows. A similar approach was employed for trade and national media monitoring with the intent to highlight stories of economic growth in US manufacturing.

The wide-ranging diversity of content formats enabled Makino to provide relevant information to social followers across all stages of the purchase decision-making process. Those nearing the point of investment were provided with convenient access to "high value" content, such as webinars and white papers, which required registration form submission. Their registration data was then added to Makino's database for direct marketing communications and sales force follow-up.

To grow social audiences and increase exposure within specific industry segments, Makino deployed several paid social programmes, including promoted content and pay-per-click (PPC) advertising.

Their journey to measuring ROI

Measurement is critical to Makino's justification for future social media investments, due in part to the manufacturing industry's slow-growing adoption of social media. When implementing the social media programme, time and monetary investment were established as the basis for comparison against other marketing efforts, with leniency granted toward key performance indicators (KPIs) that are unique to social media, such as audience growth and brand engagement. Makino tracks website referral traffic and lead generation as the primary measurements for return on investment while encouraging the sales force to report on any resulting purchases.

What they measure

Makino records and analyses data on all social media activities in order to gain a comprehensive understanding of content perform-ance and effectiveness. All social communications are directed at external audiences with an emphasis on marketing and public rela-tions content. While the company does not proactively offer customer service and support in its social media programme, user-submitted questions are accepted and answered via private messages.

Apart from ROI measurements, Makino closely tracks data on audi-ence growth, impressions, user engagement and sharing behaviour. Analysis of these KPIs enables the company to draw qualitative insights on user sentiment toward content without devoting a stren-uous amount of time and resources toward qualitative analysis of individual user responses.

How they measure

Makino takes a holistic approach to measuring its social media activities to draw valuable insights not typically seen when analyzing independent segments of data. Due to the overwhelming variety and volume of data available, Makino has designated three classifications of KPIs: Reach, Relevancy and Value. The company then evaluates all available metrics to determine those that are relevant to its established measurement classifications. The breakdown is as such:

- Reach – audience growth, post impressions, post volume.
- Relevancy – post "likes"/favourites, clicks, comments, sharing, mentions.
- Value – referral traffic, website conversions, sales leads.

The Makino team gather this data using the analytics tools and technologies offered by Facebook, Twitter, LinkedIn, YouTube and Google. Community managers use Radian6 to monitor for engagement opportunities within social discussions related to Makino or the machine tool industry.

Daily performance monitoring is performed to evaluate real-time engagement opportunities and inspect for noteworthy community reactions to content. This routine supervision is complemented by an in-depth month-to-month social media measurement report that provides a broader outlook on overall performance and community engagement. With a larger sample size of data, the company is able to identify sustainable trends that it can then react to in the following months.

Initially, the monthly report was structured to compare data segments side by side; however, Makino has found additional value from multidimensional KPIs that contrast specific data segments (e.g., impressions/post, website conversions/referral) for greater detail in performance evaluation. Each of Makino's social communities is measured independently and benchmarked against one another to identify any differing audience preferences and the relative value of each community or social network.

Makino analyses the monthly reports from multiple depths, beginning with month-to-month variations in individual KPIs. When dynamic changes are noted, the Makino team reviews any significant alterations to their social media activity that may have been performed in the previous month. They then confirm whether this variation was seen across all social communities, or unique to a specific network. Based on this information, the company then examines other KPIs within the report to identify any direct influencing factors. If a causational relationship cannot be found within the report, Makino then investigates for any uncontrolled, indirect catalysts, such as third-party websites or changes in market conditions.

The next tier of Makino's monthly reporting analysis examines results based on the company's reach, relevance and value classifications. Insights derived at this stage focus on the overall performance of each classification as well as any identifiable trends or relationships occurring between each segment.

The final stage of analysis involves a comprehensive review of social media performance results, which are then compared against other marketing activities to gauge overall value and future investment.

Example

When planning for the launch of the Make What Matters campaign, Makino recognized that it needed a strong social media component where it could connect with audiences, share campaign messages and inspire peer-to-peer dialogue. The company identified Facebook as an ideal platform to execute the campaign's initiatives based on the target audience growth and increased engagement around manufacturing conversations observed through social media monitoring.

While a Makino presence on Facebook had already been established with a corporate page, its overall activity had been limited to semi-frequent updates related to news announcements and product updates that relied on organic audience growth. In order to achieve the desired campaign objectives, the Makino team knew they had to improve the company's Facebook activity by growing the audience base and boosting engagement, while establishing clear metrics for the ROI to justify the investment. Makino set out to overcome these challenges with an integrated approach that would be supported by content marketing and social PPC advertising, enabling the company to drive rapid audience growth and nurture soft leads into sales.

The metrics for ROI on Facebook were established as referral traffic and form submissions on Makino's corporate website. The company monitored these measurements using custom reports within Google Analytics, which tracked the number of visitors who arrived at the website from Facebook, and all Facebook referrals that arrived at the company's post-form-submission web pages.

Facebook editorial calendars were developed around campaign-centric content while ensuring that each week contained multiple posts with opportunities for ROI. This was complemented by a schedule of ROI-driven promoted posts and social PPC ads to drive page "likes".

The results that Makino witnessed as a result of its Facebook efforts far exceeded initial expectations. Despite having the lowest investment cost among all of the company's campaign efforts, Facebook activities produced the highest rate of success. Year after year, the Makino team has achieved a 94 per cent increase in Facebook referral traffic to the corporate website and 107 per cent growth in website conversions. Other metrics related to campaign efforts witnessed phenomenal results with a 669 per cent increase in Makino Facebook page "likes", and a 5,541 per cent increase in Facebook post engagement.

Lessons learned

- Work closely with internal sales to determine the specifications and behaviours of a qualified lead. Share social media results and activities with the sales force and inspire them to monitor, share and participate in social discussions.
- Nurture soft leads with the support of a robust, integrated content marketing programme that maintains brand engagement from the early stages of interest to the final moment of purchase.
- Do not evaluate the success of a social media programme based on one-dimensional KPIs. Diversify measurements to gain a holistic view of performance and identify performance relationships that can be used to improve efficiency.

giffgaff – customer retention

giffgaff™

About the company

giffgaff is an MVNO (Mobile Virtual Network Operator) with roughly 75 employees, which is an incredibly small team for the industry it operates in. giffgaff breaks the mould as far as a regular business model goes for a mobile telephone operator. It is run with the help of their members who get rewarded for answering questions in the community, recruiting new members or helping to market and promote the business. This happens right the way through and includes coming up with new products and services, and helping set the direction for the company and it has seen this approach rapidly gaining traction in the mobile market. Although they can't share their annual turnover, giffgaff beats its targets of revenue, profit, customer acquisition, OIBDA, Customer Service Index, Net Promoter Score and others year after year.

The interviewee

Vincent Boon was previously giffgaff's Community Manager, but has now turned his attentions and talents to Telefónica Digital's new operating business, Standing on Giants. The B2B proposition has launched with the mission to be global leaders in serviced community management, essentially enabling businesses to access the magic ingredients that have made giffgaff such a success story since its launch in 2009.

@VincentBoon

Their social media strategy

At giffgaff the social media strategy is divided in two. On one side, there is the traditional social media channels such as Facebook, Twitter, YouTube, etc., and on the other side, there is the Forum Community. On the traditional social media side, they simply aim to provide content in a light-hearted way and do not rely on the community for this. The Forum Community platform however is different and really provides the heart and soul of the company. This is where they engage in deep discussions with their customers, or members, as they call them, on anything to do with the services and products they provide for them. The Forum Community is where giffgaff support their members to look after each other and help each other out should they encounter any problems or difficulties with the service or products. It's also the place where they look to their members to come up with tweaks and changes to what they do, all the way through to creating whole new ideas for products or services.

Traditionally Forum Communities are heavily moderated, but this is something that was changed from the beginning. Rather than moderating the members, the idea was to educate them. Although this is a relatively simple concept, the reality is anything but simple. The shift in approach to the community from the company's side was one where they looked for the positives in what the community did, rather than the negative stuff that could happen. They also embraced what the community contributed, rather than simply creating a platform where the community talked to each other. All of their processes evolved around that idea. They also continuously focused and lifted out the positive and encouraged the community as a whole to do the same. To do this effectively and at scale with hundreds of thousands of members, 17 different areas were identified in the operational model that is now used, from Behaviour Analysis through to Service Issues; from Encouragement and Reward, through to Timed Events and FAQ's. All in all, there are now well over 120 unique processes that are used to ensure the community is running well and stays a positive place for everyone to enjoy, as well as creating real value for the business.

Through using these processes, giffgaff create a real focus on a deep understanding of what the members want and need to fulfil their role within the business, as well as how they engage with the company and why. They look for long-term dialogues to ensure that highly-engaged discussions and conversations happen that contribute to the continual change within the company. They also combine the use of psychology and gamification to encourage positive contribution and work at an understanding of the sentiment that lives within the community or specific members. At times, it helps them to predict how well a specific change might go down with their members and can therefore prepare for that.

A lot of time is spent by the community team to create and sustain meaningful relationships with many different members at the same time. They also map out the different relationships members have with each other, in order to give a better understanding of how to manage the volume of people within a community. On top of this, they profile expertise and interests within the different community members to help with specific issues or questions that crop up from time to time.

Their journey to measuring ROI

Paying for a professional platform to run a community on, which has the right features and is able to deal with big fluctuations in traffic, and adding in a team to run that community, is of course not cheap. So ensuring there is a good case for ROI is very important to the business.

As any community takes a while to get established (12 months minimum), those first months are tough. So for giffgaff, part of the story was setting expectations and continuously convincing the business to put their efforts and time into the community and keeping it at the forefront of their strategies. At the same time, they had to convince the community that the community really was, and is, an integral part of the business; that they really do something with the feedback and ideas that arrive, as well as appreciate all the effort the members put in.

Once this community really starts gaining some traction, giffgaff can then look at all the different things in which it shows ROI.

What they measure

In terms of ROI, giffgaff measure quite a few things, although some are easier to get concrete results on than others. The main categories are:

- Increased Sales (number of sales directly related to the community).
- Improved Customer Service (cost reduction and customer satisfaction index).
- Product/Service Development (number of ideas coming in and implemented by the company).
- Brand Advocacy (Net Promoter Score).

- Marketing and PR (PR stories obtained through community, apps created, marketing material created, blogs written, etc.).
- Market Research (community consultations, surveys, polls, etc.).

How they measure

- **Increased Sales:** Here they look at the number of customers any other customer brings on board through their Member Get Member/affiliate programme; as well as the difference in how many customers a member of the community brings on board compared to those that are not a member of the community. Similar to any other acquisition channel they look at the Cost Per Acquisition of new customers coming in through the community.
- **Improved Customer Service:** Cost Reduction is calculated through taking a percentage of the amount of answers given by the community and the amount of views these answers get, times the average Cost Per Call, i.e., a call deflection calculation. To calculate the Continual Service Improvement, they also send out monthly surveys to a random selection of customers that have not been selected before.
- **Product/Service Development:** They look at the number of ideas coming in and the amount of comments each idea gets on average. That gives them a good idea of how good or refined the ideas are, and therefore how useful to the company they are. They also look at the amount of community ideas that get implemented by the company (one idea every three days on average so far, over two and a half years).
- **Brand advocacy:** They send out monthly surveys to a random selection of customers that have not been selected before to calculate the Net Promoter Score.

- **Marketing and PR:** They try and find PR stories through the things their community does for them. They look at the amount of applications that get created by their community and the amount of times they get downloaded, as well as the marketing material that gets created by the community, the blogs that get written by their members, and all the other things that are created for them.

- **Market Research:** They set up Community Consultations, whereby they invite their customer to take part and express their opinion on, for example, a change to a product or a new service they're thinking of launching, all the way through to a price rise they want to implement. They also run surveys and polls on a regular basis and ask their members to take part in specific research they're trying to complete.

Example

giffgaff is a low-cost company and the main thing they provide in order to make use of their service is a SIM card. This SIM card contains a chip that you put in your phone in order to receive a signal and thus the ability to make or receive calls, SMS, or data traffic. When Apple launched their iPhone and it needed a Micro SIM, this was a bit of a problem for giffgaff. It meant they had to potentially change supplier and create multiple order flows on the website. New packaging and distribution needed to get sorted out and they had to carefully consider the cost of printing and creating the Micro SIMs themselves. All this, for a relatively small base of people that would get the new iPhone. In the end it was decided that for the near future this was not something they would provide as it wasn't going to be cost effective.

Instead they worked with their community to find a solution to the problem. They started off small and one of their community members created a template which could be overlaid onto the old SIM and which showed exactly where to cut it down to size so it would fit into an iPhone and still work. People could download this template from the giffgaff website if they needed to and print it out.

SIM cutter scissors were distributed to the community so they could send them on to whichever community member needed them. The last person to receive the scissors had to send them on to the next person who wanted them.

From there a link was set up where people could ask for anyone in the community to send them a pre-cut SIM. Following that, they worked with the community to set up a full end-to-end distribution channel for any new customer that wanted a Micro SIM.

This meant the community had to build a website, add a security layer, and distribute the orders in a fair way to all the members that had signed up to do this. Once this was fully developed and working, the website was added as part of giffgaff's own order process for anyone who wanted a Micro SIM.

The end result is that hundreds of thousands of Micro SIMs have been sent out this way through the community, cutting and sending out SIMs to anyone who wants them.

Recently with iPhone5 they used the same method to send out Nano SIMs of which at least 8,000 Nano SIMs have been sent out every month through the community.

All in all this has saved giffgaff a lot of money and has given them the time they needed to slowly implement the changes without losing any customers.

Lessons learned

- Raise community awareness as much as possible within the company and without. Try and funnel all your traffic through your community to get as much traction as possible.
- Try and increase activity and participation through regular and varied incentives and use the forum not just as a self-help tool, but also a tool where you have deep and engaging discussions with your customers.
- Quantify the business benefits by defining what the key metrics and targets are and figure out what the importance to the business is. Whether that is customer service cost reductions, engagement, increased sales, an extension of the brand, use for product development etc.
- The more you integrate your community into the business processes, the more value you get out.

BRAVEday Insurance – communication

About the company

BRAVEday is an insurance advice business. The key products offered are risk products and business insurance – including shareholder protection, key person, business continuation and debt protection. Personal insurances include: medical insurance, trauma, income protection, disability and life insurance. The annual turnover of the business is $1.2 million and the business currently has seven full-time employees.

The interviewee

BRAVEday's social media owners are Ami Nathan, @aminathan and Dee Whimp, @bravedeew. Ami has been with BRAVEday for eight years and is the New Business Manager. Dee Whimp has been with BRAVEday for three years and is the Existing Business Manager. The company is very aware of the importance of continuity of the social media plan if a key employee were to leave, which is why there are two key social media owners in the company. In addition to their personal Twitter accounts, both Ami and Dee

@aminathan

jointly tweet for @BRAVEdaynz as does the Director of BRAVEday, Dean Young, who also has his own personal Twitter account, @bravedean.

@bravedeew

Their social media strategy

In the traditionally conservative, sales-focused business insurance industry, BRAVEday has always sought to stand out. Their focus on building long-term relationships, their philosophy of "being in business to help people", and their vibrant culture has helped to make social media a natural fit for the company.

Early on, BRAVEday's management saw that social media was going to be the future of client communication. Their goal was to grasp and be seen as market leaders in the industry in the social media space.

Content strategy was focused on Facebook, Twitter and LinkedIn. The company was very conscious initially to bring in external help, but consulted with social media firm syENGAGE to learn and understand social media so that eventually ownership and direction would be managed internally. The company also wanted to instil social as a business-as-usual activity and create a culture around it. This has been developed over a four-year period during which all the team are involved with two key social media drivers (Ami and Dee) who keep the process on track and managed.

Ami and Dee ensure there is always sufficient content and that the message is specific to BRAVEday's target market. The tone that BRAVEday has adopted for social media is that of "a trusted friend".

BRAVEday realizes social is not a sales tool and is a long-term commitment as a communication tool with clients and potential target market customers. Social sits well alongside the company ethos of "being in business to help people".

Involving the whole team in social makes it relevant to each team member, and prevents any one person from bearing too heavy a load. The weekly team meeting includes social media updates, and everyone contributes ideas for blog, Facebook and Twitter content.

All the team, including admins, have iPhones to make it easy and natural to share content via social.

Their journey to measuring ROI

When BRAVEday started with social media, they understood that "if we can measure it we can manage it".

The communication plan was organized to gradually move from taking guidance from external experts, to driving social from within the company. The plan was to gradually build up online presence through blogging with the goal being to have a minimum of two blogs per week, one Facebook post per day and as many Twitter interactions as possible – the key being "consistency". This was achieved by creating accountability within the team for specific actions (writing posts, increasing Twitter interactions, Facebook "likes" etc.).

Internally there was a real shift to constantly being on the lookout for content that could be used for social. From an external perspective the company was endeavouring to maintain an ongoing presence that made them the obvious "go to" people for insurance.

Again the voice of a trusted friend was critical, with the aim to communicate relevant information on insurance as well as other useful tips and information to the target market e.g., iPhone tips.

The company's tag line – "live boldly and have a brave day" is a key message.

What they measure

External

The company measures Facebook traffic, demographics, reach and engagement as well as Twitter mentions and are very interested in how many people read and share their content. Levels of engagement with Facebook competitions are also monitored. Internally, the team uses Results.com software to measure internal communication.

BRAVEday are constantly trying to improve the quality of their content as well as create content that is focused and well received by their target market. Sprout Social is used to monitor this. Other tools aren't used due to time and budget constraints.

How they measure

The BRAVEday team decided at the outset that social media was not a direct sales channel. Instead, just as with many of their other activities, they are positioning and creating conditions in which a sale can happen.

So social media, as with all other relationship- and brand-building activities, presents difficulties when trying to directly identify the "return". However the ongoing "investment" could be made a seamless part of everyday operations after some initial investment in online research, strategy development and team training.

BRAVEday also found that the activities required for maintaining external communications with potential and existing clients also lead to better internal engagement and coordination.

Example

On Facebook, BRAVEday went from "zero to hero", attracting not only a database but an increasing amount of regular client interaction.

An issue BRAVEday faced initially was that they didn't know the "how to". This problem was overcome by consulting specialists (syENGAGE). The opportunity was to communicate in a way not done well in the financial industry thereby standing out and winning the attention and interest of potential clients. Now BRAVEday's directors often hear back from the industry that they are the benchmark for social media in the insurance industry.

Costs involved were time (staff), technology (iPhones), and consultancy costs. In the view of BRAVEday's directors, the ROI is huge as they now have a whole team engaged in social. It has become part of the BRAVEday culture, business as usual, instead of something that they view as a "nice to have" operating at the side of the business.

Lessons learned

- Consistency is the key. The business needs to commit to this.
- Focus on delivering your message to your target market only (you will attract others by default).
- When you are starting out get some expert help: how to, social rules for the business and a framework to build on, this is imperative.

Beats By Dr. Dre – viral campaign

About the company

The brainchild of the artist and producer, Dr. Dre, and chairman of Interscope Geffen A&M, Jimmy Iovine, Beats comprises the Beats™ by the Dr. Dre™ family of consumer headphones, earphones and speakers, as well as Beats Audio™ software technology and streaming music subscription service Beats Music™. Through these offerings, Beats has brought the energy, emotion and excitement of playback in the recording studio to the listening experience.

The interviewee

Omar Johnson leads all global brand marketing and advertising efforts at Beats Electronics (Beats). Under his tenure, the business has grown from $180 million to a $1.1 billion dollar global icon and category leader. Before joining Beats, Omar led innovative marketing programmes for international brands including Nike, Coca-Cola and Campbell Soup.

Their social media strategy

Being social is part of the Beats™ by Dr. Dre™ DNA. The brand's focus is the artists, the fans, and the passion that people feel about music. This focus has helped drive a highly social approach to brand and product development, which has in turn powered their growth.

When they launch a new product or service, it's not enough for them to just get the product out there. They want it to become part of the current cultural conversation, and to do that, they have to invite participation. Their fans, followers and critics are as much a part of the product as their hardware and the artists they align with.

They know that self-expression and individuality are the key things to engaging with the target audience. The more ways they give the audience to express themselves, the more they pay them back with loyalty and engagement.

Example

In 2012 Beats headphones launched in a range of colours, but they didn't just want to run a TV advert to tell people about them; they wanted to create something bigger than that. They wanted to create a movement.

The launch coincided with the London Olympics 2012. Everyone in the world was going to be looking at London, so this was where they focused their efforts. Without being official sponsors it was a challenge to get a share of the London 2012 conversation, but working with digital advertising agency, R/GA London, they planned a launch campaign that would carry Beats from the Olympics in London, and around the world.

The solution

Their audience is motivated by self-expression, and by keeping that in mind Beats were able to start a conversation in London during the Olympics that would stay relevant as they launched in key cities around the globe. The #showyourcolor campaign wasn't about colour, or even about headphones; it was about individuality.

Starting with the stars of the London Olympics, they encouraged young athletes from around the world to express themselves with headphones in their national colours. The bespoke Beats #showyourcolor photo booth at London's exclusive Shoreditch House saw athletes lining up to express themselves and collect their unique headphones. Press photos from throughout the key Olympic events were dominated by the presence of Beats headphones, creating instant brand and product awareness.

Following the Olympics, the #showyourcolor message went on tour, inviting young people around the world to celebrate their individuality. The flexible system allowed the company to take the photo booth concept trialled at Shoreditch House in London, to locations around the world.

Wherever they went, from Times Square to Shanghai, the process was the same: have your photo taken, choose your colour and add your personal expression. Everyone had a chance to get involved, which is an important part of Beats as a brand. They are promoted as being made for everybody, whether you're a young person living in the suburbs or a champion on the world stage.

Away from the high-profile installations, fans were invited to join the movement on Facebook and Instagram. Participation was gathered under the hashtag #showyourcolor, creating an army of Beats fans united by self-expression. The content created inspired each new wave of fans to strive to be different.

Fuelling the conversation was the announcement that Dr. Dre would personally pick his favourite submissions to star in the next Beats™ by Dr. Dre™ TVC, alongside will.i.am and Britney Spears. This competitive element helped fans to self-moderate and curate the content they were creating.

The campaign created a mass of shareable content, including behind the scenes footage from the TV shoot and the launch of Britney and will.i.am's single, *Scream & Shout*. This helped the company to extend the conversation beyond the single world self-expression and keep it fresh and relevant for longer.

Results

The result was an additional 1.7 million fans joining the Beats Army, including a 76 per cent growth in Instagram followers and a 57 per cent increase in YouTube subscribers.

As well as a huge increase in fan base, the #showyourcolor campaign was also a commercial success. As a direct result of the campaign, Beats accounted for 80 per cent of all premium headphone sales in the US during the holiday season in 2012, plus 50 per cent of all headphone sales during the same period. Reaching 180 countries, the #showyourcolor campaign helped propel Beats by Dr. Dre to being the #1 audio brand. Most importantly, the campaign established the brand as a leader in the global culture of self-expression.

Success factors

- A high-profile launch, followed by an easily accessible participation phase.
- Having a strong story to follow gave people a reason to stay engaged.
- Beats has a distinctive tone of voice, which helps to guide the conversation.
- Ongoing content creation helped keep the campaign fresh over time.

Lessons learned

- The #showyourcolor campaign worked because it was run by a small cross-discipline team of people at Beats and the agency. As the campaign unfolded, the team were able to continually optimize the technology powering the photo booth to adapt to different needs in different locations.
- The Shoreditch House installation was essentially a prototype; as the campaign gathered momentum it was enhanced to make it faster and more robust. This way of working gave the company the flexibility to take the campaign where the conversation was, rather than having to plan everything months in advance.

PS. Are you a member yet?

Don't forget the alumni network of fellow readers, people around the world that work professionally with social media. Join by searching for "The Social Media MBA Alumni" on LinkedIn. It's free of course.

5 Safeguarding ROI

Learning Objective

The single most detrimental effect on your ROI is a crisis amplified via social channels. Ironically, the better the job you do setting everything up, the faster the news will spread, and the quicker your ROI will be impacted. However, the better you are prepared, the quicker you can diffuse the situation.

In this concluding chapter we will look at some examples of what triggered a crisis and perhaps more useful, how to prepare to deal with it.

Trying to control a social media crisis is like trying to put the genie back in the bottle. However, this does not mean that managing the crisis and taking steps to prevent a repeat isn't out of your control.

When things go wrong in social media, they tend to spiral out of control quickly. In October 2013, the social sharing start-up platform, Buffer, was hacked by a spam hack. A spam hack means that someone has accessed your account and is sending spam emails or communications to your contacts.

As to be expected, Buffer was flooded with queries and messages from their users, asking why the message was sent out. They rode out the storm by answering each and every one of the messages they received, whether they were from users or industry commentators. The speed, warmth and transparency with which they responded to their followers meant that they were able to generate positive feedback for how they managed a negative situation. Buffer used every element in their social armoury to respond to the attack – blogs, Twitter, Facebook – and also employed the traditional media to help contain the damage.

Buffer co-founder and CMO, Leo Widrich, praised his workers team spirit, "It was really incredible to see how everyone on the team just tried to find a way to help our users, whether in comments, with tweets, on Facebook and via email," he said. "I'm incredibly grateful for the people on our team and how they've responded here."

Social media crises are not the remit of the new or the small companies. Some of the most aggressive marketers in the world have been caught out by campaigns going catastrophically wrong.

McDonald's had planned to promote two hashtags back in 2012. The first, #meetthefarmers, was developed to demonstrate the fact that McDonald's are closely linked to their suppliers and uplift the idea of them using only natural products. This hashtag was in operation throughout the majority of one day, before they switched #mcdstories.

#mcdstories ran for just two hours before it was pulled. Within the two hours that it ran, #mcdstories generated a top figure of 1,600 conversations. Although there were over 70,000 general mentions of McDonald's in the same 24-hour period, there were only 2 per cent of mentions related to the #mcdstories. However, the damage that was done to the brand is still referred to today by the social media industry. The damage was two-fold:

- McDonald's instigated negative brand publicity, which means that their fans and followers are not dazzled by their notion of brand and are unable to comment negatively.
- The fact that McDonald's, who rarely put a foot wrong when it comes to marketing and who have a huge budget to assist them, got it wrong when it came to social media.

Although at first they appeared to lose control, McDonald's were able to react swiftly to nip it in the bud. However, they lost face and the damage to their reputation still lingers.

Social media crises have the capacity to become more frequent because of the nature of social media. The definition of social media is that it is a two-way conversation which means that companies are at the mercy of their fans and followers. This includes staff too.

At an Applebee's restaurant in the US, a vicar, or pastor, crossed out the pre-included 18 per cent tip, which is typically applied to parties of eight people and over, on his receipt. He then questioned why the waitress should get more than God, "I give God 10 per cent why do you get 18?" The waitress at the restaurant photographed the receipt and posted it to Reddit, but was fired for "violating customer privacy". Fans and followers saw this as a duplicitous move as Applebee's had posted a receipt with a complimentary message scribbled just weeks previously.

This story spread quickly and widely across social media platforms, with the opinion towards Applebee's becoming negative and angry.

Applebee's issued a short but defensive post on their Facebook page. This post served to add heat to the issue and generated over 10,000 further negative comments from annoyed social media users. Applebee's then responded by posting the same negative comment again and again. This created claims that Applebee's were deleting negative posts and blocking users who were being negative towards them. Applebee's continued defending itself and arguing with the online critics and within 36 hours of the original post, over 19,000 comments had been created. Applebee's then hid the original post, which generated even more bad feeling and anger within the social community. The Applebee's incident highlights the negativity which can be generated if an issue is not handled correctly – in the eyes of the users.

One way to mitigate against further damage with social media, is to create a social media crisis plan, much like a traditional crisis communications strategy:

- Create a policy which staff must adhere to. This will help control the usage and underline the importance of off-message communications.
- You should keep one ear to the air and listen to the social media chatter. Using software, like HootSuite or Radian6, ensures that you are picking up brand mentions as they happen. This is the point at which you should take the temperature of what is being said online. Determining which way the comments are leaning is critical before joining the conversation.
- Understanding what has happened and why it happened. Is this a conversation that you should be getting involved in or is it a case of least said, soonest mended?

- When the time comes to get involved, do it quickly. Speed and time are of the essence if you are to have any element in controlling how the conversation will play out. Now is the time to be honest, humble and transparent in your communications.
- Let your customers say what they have to say and then deal with it in a positive manner. Trying to stem the flow of their outbursts will reflect poorly on you as a brand. When you understand what the underlying issues are, you can begin to turn the situation to your advantage.
- Harness the negative and make it work for you. When you understand what the crux of the issue is, you are able to start to make it better with your customer. If you have done something wrong, apologize. If you're not sure who is at fault, you can afford to be magnanimous. Keep your cool with your customer and put yourself in their position when you are communicating with them. At the end of the internet is a human being. Talk to your users as you would do if you were talking to them physically.

INDEX

Index compiled by Annette Musker